To Helen

With christian love

from your old friends at
Forest Fold and the Trustees of
The Stanley Delves Trust.

John Banks

Stephen Sharpe.

John Relf.

Thos. D. Bealosh

Mr. Stanley Delves with his daughter Rachel.

PREACHING PEACE

A Biography of Stanley Delves
Pastor at Forest Fold, Crowborough, Sussex

Peter M. Rowell, B.Sc., D.Phil.
Pastor of Rehoboth Strict Baptist Chapel, Coventry

1981

Published by THE STANLEY DELVES TRUST

Distributed by ZOAR PUBLICATIONS
44 Queens Drive, Ossett, W. Yorks WF5 0ND

THE STANLEY DELVES TRUST
c/o Forest Fold Chapel, Crowborough, Sussex

© Peter M. Rowell

First Published 1981

ISBN 0 904435 46 6

Printed in England by
O.&M. Ltd., 1 Rugby Street, Leicester LE3 5FF

Contents

LIST OF ILLUSTRATIONS

PREFACE

Stanley Delves was a man who loved his Lord, and as the rich blessings of God surrounded him in his ministry he constantly insisted that all praise and honour must be given to his Saviour. The main purpose then in gathering together the 'fragments that remain' and in attempting to produce a faithful picture of his life and work, is to honour the Master he loved so deeply and served so faithfully.

My own involvement in this undertaking is simply that of a friend who was honoured by his friendship and frequently blessed by his ministry. For me his preaching was often heart-warming. I was instructed, convicted, encouraged, and comforted, but above all I found his ministry attracted my soul to the Saviour he so obviously rejoiced to preach. It is a simple but genuine testimony to say that I was always surprised and disappointed when his sermons came to an end. If my affection for the man and my regard for his ministry prevents a detached and completely objective review of his life, I can make no real apology, and believe that my feelings will be shared by all who really knew him.

From the commencement of this labour of love I have received unfailing support and encouragement from the trustees of the Stanley Delves Trust who have made this publication possible. It was their enthusiasm which stimulated so many at Forest Fold and throughout the country to write down their remembrances and to allow me to read personal letters, which have proved such an invaluable help in gaining a more detailed picture of his life. Let none feel disappointed that their contributions do not appear verbatim in the text; they have all been read and have all contributed to filling in the background and have been most helpful in the task of editing the mass of material available. I hope that those whose words *do* appear almost verbatim will take this as a grateful and sufficient acknowledgement. My task has really been that of putting together the work of others.

The Pastor at Forest Fold was also a man who loved his family and his home and I must pay grateful tribute to the way in which his two daughters, Christine and Rachel, have so willingly let me read their mother's diary, and with other relatives have allowed me to look into their family circle. The diary proved so valuable in settling dates of events and in giving that intimate touch to the record of their father's life.

I also express deep gratitude for the patient help of Miss Eunice

Kirk and many others who have deciphered my writing and spent many hours in typing and retyping the manuscript.

It is my prayer that the writing of this book will, in some small way, continue the work for which Stanley Delves spent his life - to preach the Lord Jesus Christ as the only Saviour of lost sinners and to magnify the grace of God in the experiences of those who love Him.

Coventry. August 1981

PUBLISHER'S NOTES

The Trustees of the Stanley Delves Trust wish lovingly to acknowledge the untiring work of the author, Dr. Peter Rowell, Pastor of Rehoboth Chapel, Coventry, in the preparation of this book - the life of Stanley Delves.

Although already heavily committed to pastoral, ministerial and editorial work, in late 1978 he willingly responded to our desire that he would undertake this labour of love. With the volume now finished, we believe by God's guidance we could not have made a better choice.

We also acknowledge, from the outset, the guidance and the ever available help of our esteemed friend Mr. David Oldham of Stamford, upon whom we have so heavily relied at all stages of this work.

As Trustees, we are very grateful to all the kind friends who in so many different ways have made this book possible.

May our blessed God 'Preach Peace' into the souls of those who read these pages.

1

The Beginning
1897-1912

"Though thy beginning was small, yet thy latter end should greatly increase".

Job 8.7.

It is still true that "not many wise men after the flesh, not many mighty, not many noble are called: but God hath chosen the foolish things of the world to confound the wise, and God hath chosen the weak things of the world to confound the things which are mighty; and base things of the world, and things which are despised, hath God chosen, yea, and things which are not, to bring to nought things that are: that no flesh should glory in his presence". The fishermen of Galilee who received that gracious and urgent call from the Saviour's lips, "Follow me", were the first in a long and honoured line of faithful preachers of the Word, so many of whom have been chosen from the most obscure and unlikely environment. Lacking the aristocratic pedigree, the celebrated name, and the wealth of this world they are, nevertheless, called to be "ambassadors for Christ". They bear His name, come with His credentials, and though amongst the poor of this world, they are rich in faith and heirs of a kingdom which is not of this world. Such was the man whose humble, God-honouring, and Christ-exalting life is now to be sketched.

It was in the small Sussex village of Rushlake Green on 28 November 1897 that Stanley Delves was born. This attractive village is situated about three miles south-east of Heathfield and falls within the parish of Warbleton where the local church has strong connections with Richard Woodman, the Sussex iron-maker who was martyred at Lewes in 1557 during Queen Mary's reign. A plaque can be seen in memory of this godly man in the wall of the churchyard.

In Warbleton, at the end of the nineteenth century, there were three distinct social classes, seemingly as fixed as the church tower; the upper, aristocratic class consisting of two local families; the Dunns, living at Stone House, and the Darbys, of Marklye. Their impressive homes can still be seen not far from the village of

Rushlake Green, and it was they who owned most of the land around the village. So distinct was their social position that they even had their own door into the church and reserved pews for their exclusive use. The second group were the middle class of yeoman farmers and craftsmen which included Stanley's father, the village blacksmith, and his uncle, the village carpenter and wheelwright. Lastly, there were the labourers who were wholly dependent on the two other groups both for their homes and livelihood.

Most villages in those days were almost self-sufficient, and it was considered somewhat less than loyal to leave the local traders and go elsewhere. The Warbleton miller hardly dare go up to London dressed in the customary top hat for the City to buy imported "hard wheat", for fear that local farmers would hear of his journey, so he would carry his top hat in a brown paper bag and go to the railway station wearing his cap, making a discreet change en route. Stanley recalled many aspects of village life in later years, remembering the annual fair on the village green which must have seemed very much like Bunyan's "Vanity Fair" but very attractive to a young boy whose home was virtually on the edge of the green. He also remembered the annual occasion when all the local farmers assembled at the village Inn to pay their rents and were treated to a very satisfying meal by the local landowners. The buildings which were once the blacksmith's forge can still be seen beside the local garage, and the impressive house where Stanley was born still stands in front of the forge.

Stanley's parents, Jonah and Fanny Delves, were simple country folk, and his birth was unnoticed by all the world except the few who were so intimately concerned. To them, however, the event was an answer to many prayers; another precious life was brought safely into the world and they now had a family of four boys – Edgar, Jesse, Nelson, and lastly Stanley. The joy of that home was very real and had a depth which many never experienced, for this baby's parents were both true believers in their Saviour, Jesus Christ. They knew that God was the Giver of every good gift and it was to Him they turned in praise and thankfulness, committing the life of their fourth and last child to the Lord Who had so richly blessed them. The children of this home were surrounded with loving prayers, wise scriptural counsel, and a practical example of real yet simple Christianity. Jonah Delves, the village blacksmith, had a loyal, active wife who helped with the family expenses by making butter in the old fashioned way with a churn worked by hand. It was, then, a very simple home into which Stanley was born and in these plain surroundings he spent a most happy childhood.

Stanley, recalling his early life at a much later date, said:

I had not the advantages now provided for children and young people to equip themselves, nor was I very desirous of them, for I had no idea of any prominence in life nor any ambitions whatever.

Though their education was limited and elementary, at least two of the family, Jesse and Stanley, proved in a striking way that where there is natural ability, encouragement, and diligence, it is possible to reach a level of knowledge and understanding far beyond that of the simple teachers of early years. Both these sons became respected Christian ministers with a wide knowledge of secular and religious history and a deep grasp of true theology.

Although he was quite upset when, in later years, the village school in Rushlake Green was pulled down, Stanley never enjoyed school. Perhaps this was partly because he was a late developer as far as academic learning was concerned, but possibly more because of uninteresting methods of schoolteaching in those days. His interest always lay in finding out things for himself. He found history the only interesting subject at school and never was any good at spelling.

It is essential in considering the development of spiritual life in any of God's children to pay the closest attention to their early environment. True religion in any soul is indeed a sovereign work of the Holy Spirit and certainly not merely the effect of early influences as some modern psychologists would suggest. Nevertheless, God graciously works through a whole variety of means to accomplish His own purposes. Believing parents take very much to heart their wedding promise to bring up their children in the nurture and admonition of the Lord, and the Apostle Paul tells us of the influence on Timothy of the faith of his mother and grandmother, so that from a child he had known the Holy Scriptures which are able to make one "wise unto salvation". Such influences were strong in the blacksmith's home in Rushlake Green. The Bible was always in evidence; daily reading of the Word and prayer by father would have been the invariable practice. In the account of the life of Stanley's brother, Jesse, published in the *Gospel Standard* in January 1981, Jesse recalled these early days:

Through mercy I was blessed with consistent and God-fearing parents, setting before us as a family a good example, training us in the fear of the Lord, in truth and uprightness. I often reflect upon the days of my childhood with thankfulness to the Lord for this blessing, daily reading and prayer with the family present whenever convenient, his children always having a warm place in my father's petitions at the throne of grace.

Jonah Delves was deacon of the church meeting at Mount Hermon Chapel. This small Strict Baptist chapel is situated to the north of the village of Rushlake Green and is most aptly named, for the family had a long uphill walk to their chapel which is actually situated in the parish of Warbleton. The surroundings are completely rural and as one ascends to the chapel there is a constantly expanding view over Rushlake Green across the beautiful Sussex countryside towards the much larger town of Hailsham and the Sussex coast.

It is not difficult to imagine the pattern of life in a family with these religious connections. Theirs was a home in which the husband loved the wife and the wife submitted willingly to her husband; a home where life was regulated in an orderly way but certainly not in a harsh or repressive way. The focal point of each week was the Lord's day, which was regarded indeed as a day apart. Even on Saturday preparations would be made, clean clothes laid ready for the morning and children's shoes cleaned. As much of the preparation of food as possible was a Saturday task and all in order that the Lord's day might be a day of rest and freedom to worship God in the way beloved by such Protestant Nonconformists.

These godly country folk were Baptists by conviction, firmly believing the Baptist independent church order to be scriptural but, more importantly, believing in the precious truths of a free grace gospel. There were three principal aspects to the religious teaching with which these people were surrounded.

Firstly, there was a strong emphasis upon Scripture as the Word of God in its entirety, and flowing from that conviction a consistent proclamation of the doctrines of free and sovereign grace. The great foundation truths of the Reformation and the strong influence of Puritan theology and practice were the lifeblood of the weekly preaching in such Sussex chapels.

Secondly, in the simple preaching they heard, there was an insistent reminder of the need for a personal experience of the sovereign work of the Holy Spirit in regeneration. The text beloved by George Whitefield, "Ye must be born again" was a theme repeated in many different ways from these plain pulpits. This was united to a strong emphasis upon the varied aspects of Christian experience; conviction of personal sin and spiritual need, a real "call by grace", a true conversion in turning from sin to the living God, sincere repentance evidenced by a real change in a person's way of life, a new spirit of separation from an unbelieving world and its sinful pleasures, but above all, and as the source of all this, a deeply personal relationship of loving faith in the only Saviour of sinners as He was revealed to the heart by the Holy Spirit. This personal experience of salvation they believed was to be followed by a public confession of faith to the church members and then by a demonstration of that faith in their obedience to the Saviour's command to be baptized. These baptized believers were then welcomed as members of the local church.

Thirdly, these people were deeply concerned about the life and witness of their local church. They maintained a scriptural discipline so that all who erred in doctrine or who were guilty of moral failures knew that they would have to answer to the church for such lapses unless there were clear signs of repentance. This laid a healthy restraint, not a legal bondage, upon all church members as they were consistently encouraged to live a godly life giving proof of their spiritual standing as the elect of God. These churches knew that free grace does not lead to licentiousness and that the liberty of the Gospel is not a licence to sin.

Whilst aware of the church of God in its widest aspect, these country folk lived in a day when travel and communication were slow. This led to an intense concern for that part of God's work in the earth which concerned them most. They certainly avoided the pitfall of a vague universalism even if they strayed sometimes into too limited a view of God's work in the world at large. However, their committment to their own chapel was wholehearted, their buildings were erected and maintained from their own weekly giving and their ministers paid (not over generously in some cases!) from the same source without any financial help from outside funds. Such local church concern gave rise to a closely knit church community in which the Apostle's injunction to "exhort one another daily" was taken to heart. The numerical strength of the church and its impact on the local community was a matter of real concern even in those days when "churchgoing" was so much more common than today. The strength of nominal religion still deeply affected life in England at this time, but in Sussex it seems that there was a very great deal of religion which was much more than nominal.

This family lived, then, in an atmosphere where the great concerns of eternity, of man's relationship with God, of God's will for men, of a truly Christian life, of the certainty of death, of the certainty of a future heaven or hell and of the pre-eminence of Christ, were constantly before them. Such an environment God undoubtedly used in the lives of Jesse and Stanley to mould many of their lifelong attitudes, convictions and associations.

During the whole of his life and particularly as he grew older, Stanley recalled the happy memories of his simple village childhood; taking the butter made by his mother for sale round the village; playing with his school friends; growing and selling marrow plants; keeping rabbits; tickling trout in the nearby millpond, and doing all the things which lively boys still love to do in the freedom of the countryside. He told of a lesson learned amidst these pleasures which he never forgot. A friend had some rabbits for sale and he went to buy one of them. Handing over his sixpence he went to choose his rabbit, but the friend had other ideas and he found that having parted with his money he had to accept what he was given and had not been allowed a free choice!

Annual family holidays in those days were impossible for many because of the cost, but this was more than recompensed for young Stanley as he had a favourite cousin, Arthur Miles, the son of his mother's sister, who lived in Eastbourne. The distance from Rushlake Green to Eastbourne was only twenty miles but travel was much slower then, usually by horse and cart, and it was on the carrier's cart which took his mother's butter to Eastbourne for sale that the excited lad went for his holidays by the sea. It is not really strange that for most people those golden days of youthful summer holidays were times when the sun always seemed to shine and some adventurous plan was always in prospect. Certainly it was so for the two friends in Eastbourne. On one occasion they found a live crab which was soon named 'Jack Apple'. The poor creature had to be taken home but sadly, though not surprisingly, it died in transit. 'Jack Apple' had to be graced with a funeral in the back garden, being buried in a match box. The funeral service was conducted by young Stanley, who often said, "When I grow up I shall be a minister and wear a black alpaca jacket".

On Sundays the boys attended Grove Road Strict Baptist Chapel, where the Pastor in those days was Henry Bradford, much loved by his congregation and greatly respected by local people. Although neither of the boys was as yet converted they were affected in a natural way by the gentle, Christ-like spirit of the Pastor. There was a large congregation and a correspondingly large Sunday School at

Grove Road. Several of the boys were killed a few years later during the 1914-18 war, and these included Arthur's brother Herbert. Of those who survived, almost all became useful members of churches; deacons, ministers, and pastors. One of the boys, Reginald Honeysett, became Pastor of Providence Chapel, Cranbrook, and was a lifelong friend of both Arthur and Stanley.

By his own admission, Stanley was an adventurous and lively youth, and both he and Arthur found it hard to sit still through the Sunday services. This problem was resolved by the Sunday School Superintendent who was wont to prod restless children with a long pole normally used to light the gas lamps! After a week by the sea, Stanley would return by the carrier's cart, Arthur going too, on an exchange visit to the country.

Grove Road church sent out several ministers to preach during that period and sometimes they travelled with the boys by cart on the Saturday. Often the minister stayed with the Delves family before preaching on the Sunday at Mount Hermon Chapel, and as this was before the days of the telephone, Mrs. Delves welcomed the opportunity to hear news of her relatives in Eastbourne from the minister.

Holidays at Rushlake Green were just as lively as at Eastbourne, which is hardly surprising as there were no girls in either family. A girl cousin, Kitty, was one of their playmates. Disaster appears to have overtaken her on one occasion when, dared by the boys, she started to walk along a fence by the side of the village pond. Stanley's brother, Jesse, began to walk from the other end and they met in the middle where they attempted to pass, but Kitty fell in. Mercifully, the consequences were no worse than a very wet Kitty!

Mount Hermon chapel with its Sunday School evidently played a very significant part in Stanley's childhood and early youth. He used to relate with obvious pleasure that he was born while his father was attending morning service there. As he grew older his involvement at the chapel increased and for a period he played the organ. It became his habit to remain behind after the afternoon service whilst his mother provided tea for the visiting ministers before they returned home. He recounted how he used to listen to the conversation between his mother and the minister as he waited quietly at the bottom of the vestry steps, always managing to creep away in time so that his eavesdropping was never noticed. Later on in the day he would laugh to himself when he heard his mother telling his father the minister's news, suitably disguised (as she thought) from his apparently uninterested ears. He always considered that these overheard conversations formed his early initiation into some of the problems which arise in churches and among ministers.

It was a source of real regret later in life that he could not remember more of the sermons of the gracious men who preached at Mount Hermon during these early years, but certainly they left their mark both on the style of his own preaching method and particularly on that often imperceptible beginning of spiritual concern as God begins to open the heart to the truth of the Gospel. One of the most solemn services at Mount Hermon made a lifelong impression on them all, for on 7 April 1907, when he was only nine years old, he remembers how Mr. Pope the minister was announcing Hymn No.992 *(Gadsby's)* when he suddenly collapsed and died.

During those years at Rushlake Green he had, with his three brothers, a very strong attachment to his mother, and she undoubtedly had a profound influence on his development into manhood. He recounted how his later visits to Bodle Street chapel reminded him of those early years when he would walk the three miles from Rushlake Green after school on the days of the special services at Bodle Street, simply to have the pleasure of walking home with his mother after the evening service.

Over sixty years later, when reviewing this period of his life, he wrote:

> My early life gives me little pleasure as I remember it, for though I was under a gracious parental upbringing and regularly attended Chapel and Sunday School I can only say with the Psalmist, 'Remember not the sins of my youth ... according to thy mercy remember thou me for thy goodness' sake, O Lord.' But at times I was not without solemn feelings and resolutions to be better; but these wore off, and I thought that when I was free to do so I would go my own way. There were evils in my heart which would have been my eternal ruin had sovereign grace not intervened.

On 3 June 1972, Mr Delves was persuaded to give some account of his life and Christian experience to his own church and congregation, and so from his own lips we have a brief account of the first stirrings of that concern which lead on to spiritual life:

> The earliest religious impressions that I can remember were under hearing the minstry of the late Mr. Botten of the Dicker. There was something about Mr. Botten's ministry that alarmed me. I cannot remember anything particular that he said but, in some way, when I heard Mr. Botten preach, and he used to come to our anniversary at our little Mount Hermon Chapel, I would be quite alarmed about death and the judgement so that often I had a very bad night after I heard Mr. Botten preach. But this preaching

conveyed to me no idea whatever of the Gospel, it just alarmed me. It set off a concern about my soul without giving me any instruction with regard to the way in which my soul could be saved. These feelings used to come and go. Sometimes I would be in a real terror about my soul and then that would pass off and I would be very careless and thoughtless and I must say that looking back over my early years, there is very little that gives me any pleasure to remember. I do not know that I really ran into downright sin but still there is much that causes me to say even now as I think about it, "Remember not the sins of my youth, nor my transgressions: according to thy mercy remember thou me for thy goodness' sake, O Lord." Ps. 25.7. I can look back now and see enough to know where things would have led me had I been left to the way of my own heart. Still, there was started off in this way of being alarmed about the judgement and eternity, a concern about my soul. On review I feel that my soul *was* quickened because desires after spiritual things developed from those early alarms and impressions, though I had then no saving faith in Jesus Christ.

It was in this unsettled state of mind and heart that Stanley had to face the first great change in his life, a change which took him from the quiet rustic way of life in Rushlake Green to the bustling activity of a shop assistant's life in Tunbridge Wells.

2

The Obedience of Faith
1912-1914

"Now unto him that is of power to stablish you according to my gospel, and the preaching of Jesus Christ, according to the revelation of the mystery, which was kept secret since the world began, But now is made manifest, and by the scriptures of the prophets, according to the commandment of the everlasting God, made known to all nations for the obedience of faith: To God only wise, be glory through Jesus Christ for ever. Amen."

Romans 16.25-27.

Formal education came to an early conclusion in Stanley's life and as he approached the age of fifteen there were serious debates as to his future. He never spoke of having formed any definite ambitions for his life, as he lived at a time when parents usually made such decisions for their children's future, probably because these decisions had to be made when the children were not old enough to know their own minds on such matters. It was decided that Stanley was to join his brother Edgar in the Police Force, but being too young to commence his training, his brother managed to find work for him in Tunbridge Wells. To move away from home and parents at the early age of fifteen years and to face the responsibilities of earning a living is not a common occurrence today but this was the prospect which Stanley had now to contemplate. Only those who know the comfort of close family relationships and a truly happy Christian home can imagine the feelings of one so young as he left his parents to live with strangers in a strange home. It had been arranged that he should live with and work for a Mr. J. W. Harmer of Tunbridge Wells, who was both a grocer by trade and also a very useful itinerant preacher at weekends. The change in environment was not therefore so great as it might have been as he went to lodge in a home where Christian principles prevailed.

The Psalmist, David, expresses a simple but precious truth when he declares "My times are in thy hand" Ps. 31.15, and all true believers will say the same as Ryland in his well known hymn:

"Sovereign Ruler of the skies,
Ever gracious, ever wise;
All my times are in Thy hand,
All events at Thy command."

Birthplace of Stanley Delves as it appears today.

A corner of Rushlake Green.

Mount Hermon Chapel, where the Delves' family attended for worship

The Pantiles, Tunbridge Wells.

Certainly this development in Stanley's life was one of those special events which affected the whole of his future, for in the home of Mr. and Mrs. Harmer he met their daughter, Esther Caroline, who eventually became his wife. He later described this deeply significant event in one short sentence:

There I met his daughter, Esther Caroline, who subsequently became my precious and faithful wife.

Their first introduction, however, was not very auspicious as the Harmer grocery business had had a succession of unsatisfactory shop boys, and Esther Caroline did not much welcome the arrival of yet another! Evidently this initial reaction was soon revised, and a growing friendship developed between them which issued in their marriage twelve years later, but, as so often is the case, the course of true love did not run smooth, and they were both to find their friendship tested in the fires of trial. The family he had come to live with had many concerns beyond those of the grocery business. Mr. Harmer carried the burden of the ministry of the Word which took him away from home every Lord's day to preach mainly in local Particular Baptist Chapels, leaving his wife to care for a crippled son, Ebenezer, who was a hunchback and confined to a wheelchair. To add to their troubles, Esther was not a strong girl and she suffered a good deal of ill-health from an early age.

The Harmer's new shop-boy however proved to be diligent and very interested in the business, and Stanley himself soon began to feel that his future lay in the grocery trade rather than the Police Force. One feature of the new shop assistant which much impressed his employer was that he was the first of their shop boys who wanted to attend a place of worship, and for a while he went with them to Hanover Strict Baptist Chapel in the centre of Tunbridge Wells. In the good providence of God we have a record of the development of Stanley's spiritual concerns through this period in his own words:

In due time I came to Tunbridge Wells to live, and I was then about 15 or 16 years of age. By that time my concern had settled down into a seeking after the knowledge of the truth. I felt I wanted to know the truth and to believe the truth, but I felt very ignorant and very confused and, as you have heard me say, about that time my prayer so often was (and it was really the prayer of my heart and the confession of my heart) - "Lord, I feel so ignorant, I do not seem to know what to believe, I do not seem to know what the truth is, I do not even seem to know what it is to believe. Do teach me. Do show me the truth". Well, in that way I used to attend the ministry of Mr. Newton at Hanover Chapel. I had a very great regard for Mr. Newton. I felt he was a very venerable servant of the Lord, but somehow his preaching did not seem to have much effect on my own heart. It was not because I had no concern, because at that time in my life I used to pray my way along the street to Chapel, asking that the Lord would bless my soul, but still nothing seemed to come with any particular power to me. However, one Sunday morning I got to Hanover Chapel very early, too early to go into the service, so I felt I would go for a walk on the common. I was so lost in my thoughts and ponderings in these matters that I came to realise that at 11 o'clock I was at the bottom of the common. I thought "Well, if I go back to Hanover I shall be very late for the service", so I went into Rehoboth.* Mr. Evans, the Pastor, was then preaching, and I remember that Mr. Evans' ministry had an effect on me that I had never felt before. There seemed a power in it that affected me and held me and so I went again in the evening. If I remember right, Mr. Evans was then preaching on the sufferings of Jesus Christ. It was not that I could understand things very clearly but there seemed to be a power in his preaching that I had not felt before, which of course attracted me to his ministry. So I commenced to attend Rehoboth Chapel.

At about that time a friend lent me a book on "The Passover as a Type of the Lord Jesus Christ". As I read this and pondered over it, and especially these words in it "And the blood shall be to you for a token,.... and when I see the blood I will pass over you", I verily believe the Holy Spirit began to enlighten my understanding and the first ray of Gospel light that ever shone into my confused mind and spirit was through that Scripture. In that light I saw the heart of the Gospel to be the substitution of Jesus Christ in the sinner's place, bearing away his sin. It was made to appear to me that the blood was a token that there had been death in that house, the death of the lamb, and where there had been the death of the lamb there would not be the death of the firstborn. It was because of the blood, the sign of the death of the lamb, that the firstborn was preserved from the fateful stroke that night.

So I began to see the Gospel truth of substitution, that it was really this - it was "Jesus in the sinner's place". Now as I saw that, so I believed it. My heart responded to that wonderful truth, and this was the feeling and response which my heart felt to that truth:

"Go, ye that rest upon the law,
And toil and seek salvation there,
Look to the flame that Moses saw,
And shrink, and tremble, and despair.

But I'll retire beneath the Cross;
Saviour, at thy dear feet I'll lie!
And the keen sword that Justice draws,
Flaming and red, shall pass me by.   *Watts*

Well now, that teaching and that light and that revelation brought my very heart to believe in the precious blood of Jesus Christ as a substitute for sin. I do not know that it brought me an assurance with regard to my own sins being pardoned, so much as showing me the way of God's mercy. It was

*This is another Strict Baptist chapel situated only a few yards from the Pantiles in Tunbridge Wells.

through the substitutionary sacrifice of Jesus Christ, because I had never seen that, although of course I had heard of Jesus Christ all my early days. I remember I came to Tunbridge Wells when I was in this concern of mind, and a minister (it was in fact our Mr. Relf's grandfather who used occasionally to preach at the chapel) raised this question, as to how God could be just and forgive sin. Well, I knew I felt God was just and very holy - there was no mistake about that in my mind. I knew that I was sinful and I felt that, and it seemed to me as though it was a straight issue between the sinfulness of my heart and the holiness and the justice of God. I could not see any way out of it. But I remember Mr. Relf made this remark, "Well, it is through the doing and the dying of the Lord Jesus" and there he left it. He did not explain it. Well, I listened but I could not see what the doing and the dying of the Lord Jesus had to do with it. It seemed to me that the crux of the matter was the holiness of God and the sinfulness of my nature. I think we ministers make a mistake in thinking that our congregations so understand the elementary principles of the Gospel that there is no need for us to expound them. That is a mistake. It would have been very helpful to me if that good minister had expounded the point as to how "the doing", as he called it, and "the dying" of the Lord Jesus Christ could be of any blessing to me. But I saw it so clearly afterwards. O, in that precious blood I saw it. I saw how my soul could be saved, how God could be holy, just, and yet kind, loving, tender and merciful, and my heart responded to it. And so I came to believe in Jesus Christ and His precious blood, and to shelter my soul believingly beneath His protection. I was then, I suppose, about 16 or 17 years old. There I was then; there I am today. There I hope to live and there I hope to die, sheltered beneath that precious blood.

Well, as I came to believe these things in my heart so I began to feel the blessing of the Gospel. I began to feel that sweet, that holy, and that heavenly peace which comes by the blood of the Cross. And it was sweet to me too! My soul lived in it. Words like this, for instance, would be very much my feelings:

> "Sweet the moments, rich in blessing,
> Which before the Cross I spend."

or this:

> "Here it is I find my heaven,
> While upon the Lamb I gaze."   *Allen & Batty*

And I did spend them and they were rich to my soul. I felt the peace of God to be heavenly and I enjoyed the services. The Lord's house and the Lord's people were very attractive to me, and I developed a very great love for Rehoboth Chapel. I remember once coming away down the little passage from the chapel and stopping and turning round and looking at the chapel and that word coming to me, "Thy servants take pleasure in her stones and favour the dust thereof".* I felt a love to every stone of the place. Well, being thus brought into the knowledge of the Gospel and feeling the blessing of it in my soul, I went along very comfortably for a while. I enjoyed

*Psalm 102. 14

the ministry; the Word preached was mixed with faith in my heart in hearing it, and I profited by it accordingly. I always look back on those days as my good hearing days. They really were *my* hearing days. I have not had the like since, but then I fed on the Word.

Well, as time went on, with these feelings in my heart, I became concerned about baptism. For one thing, baptisms were very frequent at Rehoboth in those days, and the Pastor gave a certain prominence to baptism in his ministry, and I accordingly became concerned with regard to this matter. I wanted to do what was right. So I betook myself to praying over this question and asking the Lord to show me that it was right for me to be baptized. But I never seemed to get very far with that nor to feel very much access to the Lord about it, until it was made to appear to me that the Lord had already shown me in His Word that it was right for me to be baptized — on this principle — that baptism was appointed for all believers in Jesus Christ. It seemed to me then that I was setting aside the plain direction of the scripture and looking for some special direction from the Lord. And that so wrought on my mind that I became quite unable to pray about it at all. It seemed to me that I was setting aside the plain direction which the Lord had given to all believers. It is not the Lord's will that some believers should be baptized and not others. If that were the case, we would need a special and individual direction from the Lord about it. But when it is the Lord's will for all believers, what ground have we to expect that He will give us some special, individual and personal direction? Well, I was constrained by love and so I came forward and made application to be baptized. But just at this juncture I must say that you will not understand all the tensions of mind that I subsequently went through, unless you appreciate that unhappily I am a man of a very fearful heart and extremely averse to publicity, and I still am, in my natural disposition, very retiring. The thought of having to speak before the Church seemed to be such an ordeal, and I remember before I went into the Church meeting, I was waiting all in a shake and a tremble, and my spirit rather rebelled against it. I remember saying, "Why can't we follow the Lord in this way without being subject to such a strain and such an ordeal as this?" However, I did speak, but I hardly know how. I was received and, of course, baptized. I never felt any particular blessing in my baptism. Certainly nothing like I have felt from time to time in baptizing others. But still, I felt that I had taken the right step. I felt that in my heart I believed in Jesus Christ. I loved His name, His truth and His ways. So I was baptized and commenced my public confession of my faith in Jesus Christ, and all that I have been through since has never once made me wish that I had not taken that step.

How fervently the Apostle Paul prays for the Ephesian believers (Eph. 1.17-18) "That the God of our Lord Jesus Christ, the Father of glory, may give unto you the spirit of wisdom and revelation in the knowledge of him: The eyes of your understanding being enlightened; that ye may know what is the hope of his calling, and what the riches of the glory of his inheritance in the saints, And what is the exceeding greatness of his power to us-ward who believe, according to the working of his mighty power". This mighty power Stanley had now experienced, and that first work of regeneration or new birth had become evident in his public confession of Jesus Christ and his membership of the church at Rehoboth, Tunbridge Wells. In a very distinct way the heart of Gospel truth had been revealed to him so that in his own soul the substitutionary, atoning work of Jesus, the Lamb of God, was like a foundation on which the rest of his Christian life and ministry rested. His understanding had indeed been enlightened in a way which is vitally necessary for all true believers, but also in that special way which is essential for those called to minister the Word of life and to be ambassadors for Christ.

During the whole of this period of spiritual establishment he was working for Mr. Harmer and living with the family, and it is evident that his friendship with Esther Caroline was deepening apace. Esther kept a personal diary intermittently from 1914 to 1955 and these diaries have proved a most valuable source of information about their friendship, courtship and married life. Also revealed there is the fascinating story of the growth of another spiritual life, fashioned by the hands of the Heavenly Potter, as a "vessel unto honour" (Rom. 9.21). This vessel was being produced through the fires of temptation, physical weakness and pain, so that Esther could eventually be an understanding and true helpmeet for her husband in his life's work, and whilst this is not Esther's biography it is the biography of a man whose life was profoundly affected by what God was doing, and would do, in her life. One of the earliest notes in her diary on 3 February 1914 was a sad omen of the future:

Doctor says I shall have to lay up again.

And then on 9 February:

Have had to start lying in bed again but I feel more reconciled knowing "My Father's hand prepares the cup, and what He wills is best".

This constant trouble with ulcerated legs was a lifelong burden and, though greatly used by God for her sanctification, was the cause of her sad death in 1963.

During 1914 Esther and Stanley spent much time together when not working in the shop, for on 8 March Esther records a significant development:

Stanley and I have started morning reading and are going through the epistles.

Although four years older than Stanley, she was a few steps behind him in the spiritual pathway. He was already a church member at

15

Rehoboth and a series of entries during this year tell of her concerns about being baptized and joining the church which they both attended regularly. It is clear that she was already spiritually alive, that she had a spiritual appreciation of the gospel ministry and was much concerned to do the will of her God. She eventually asked her Pastor, Mr. Evans, if she could be baptized, but so great was the subsequent turmoil of mind that she had to tell him that she could not speak to the church and give her testimony. On 11 July she comments:

"I am feeling so wretched and miserable and have such a spirit of infidelity in me that I have written to Mr. Evans to say I cannot go before the church".

In spite of continuing turmoil of mind, she was eventually baptized in March 1917 and became a member at Rehoboth, so that both she and Stanley were united in the truth of the Gospel and in church membership at least seven years before they eventually married.

By July of 1914 the Great War had commenced and Esther records much of the confusion and concern of those sad days:

1 Aug.	The war trouble in Europe is looking very black now.
2 Aug.	War has broken out in full force.
4 Aug.	We were very busy all day, people getting scared about the war and prices going up.
6 Aug.	There was a special prayer meeting on behalf of the nation at 'Hanover'.
14 Aug.	H., Ebb and I went to the Y.P.U. room to work for the soldiers H. cut out shirts, Ebb helped to roll bandages, and I cut up the calico ready for the bandages.

On 24 September Stanley moved from Harmer's grocery business to take a position with another local grocer, Durrants, whose shop was on the Pantiles in Tunbridge Wells. It was here that he worked until after his marriage, apart from his short period in the army, but his move from the Harmer home evidently did not affect his friendship with Esther, for on 13 December she briefly states:

Stanley brought me home at night.

A gracious God was surely guiding and blessing two young people who had put their trust in Him, two young believers who were seeking first the kingdom of God and His righteousness, proving yet again the truth of His own promise, "Them that honour me I will honour". I Sam. 2.30.

3

Preach the Word
1914-1920

"How then shall they call on him in whom they have not believed? and how shall they believe in him of whom they have not heard? and how shall they hear without a preacher? and how shall they preach, except they be sent? as it is written, How beautiful are the feet of them that preach the gospel of peace, and bring glad tidings of good things!"

Romans 10.14-15.

How often it is that a sovereign God has prepared those He has chosen for the work of the ministry in the fiery trials of loneliness, spiritual distress, and deep soul exercise. Elijah, though already a prophet, learned much in the deserts of Arabia and even more at the door of the cave in the mount of Horeb: I Kings 19. Centuries later Paul follows a similar path and tells the Galatians "Neither went I up to Jerusalem to them which were apostles before me; but I went into Arabia". Gal. 1.17.

Stanley was only seventeen when the First World War commenced and it was not long before the calm and pleasantness of life in Tunbridge Wells was rudely threatened. He was called up for national service but, due to some physical condition, he was at first rejected. However he was not to escape the trial of war service. As the war progressed and the flower of Britain's youth was decimated in the bloodstained trenches of Europe, so the demand for more men to fill the empty places meant that those who had first been rejected had to face the rigours of a war in which eight and a half million soldiers, sailors, and airmen were killed. It was in 1917, when he was nineteen, that Stanley had to leave all he loved in England and especially in Tunbridge Wells, and the following details of his wartime experiences have been gleaned from his writing and reminiscences:

When I entered military service I was stationed near to Canterbury for some months and from there I went to the south of Ireland. I was attached to a mobile unit and travelled to Dublin, Limerick, and in both the north and south of Ireland. Here I saw what the Roman Catholic church was at first hand; I saw both the poverty of the people and the power of the Roman Catholic religion over them. From Ireland I was sent to Archangel in

Northern Russia and was there for twelve months and had ample time to observe the Greek Orthodox religion. Although the latter repudiates some of the practices of the former, I saw little to choose between them. Most of the time in Russia was spent by the River Dvina and all through one winter, so I knew what the severity of an arctic winter was. I was preserved from some mysterious dangers there whilst others who were with me lost their lives. I will mention just one of a number of occasions when the Lord preserved me from death which I feel would certainly have befallen me if the Lord had not overruled my circumstances.

When I was in Archangel I was attached as a signaller to a unit with an officer, and the whole company was detailed to go on a certain expedition. But I was taken from them because another signaller needed a signaller more than the one that I had been attached to, so I and the Captain were sent on another expediton from which we safely returned, but the other company to which I really belonged and the other officer had run into an ambush. They were nearly all massacred and the officer I had served was amongst them — I never saw him again — he was dead and nearly all those who were with him. Humanly speaking, if I had not been taken from him and attached to another officer, it would have been my end, for hardly any of the company came out of that danger alive.

In the manner which is common to most soldiers, Stanley sometimes told of other incidents relating to this period in Russia. On one occasion he and a friend were in a hut on a hillside which came under attack. He ran out of the hut and up the hillside but his friend ran down the hill only to be killed instantly by a shell. He said that he felt to be sovereignly preserved and was filled with most solemn feelings as he gave thanks to God for his escape.

This period amidst such danger and in such extremes of climate was one in which his faith was severely tested, and he tells of this time of trial:

Now all the time I was in Russia I was in a very dark and desolate state spiritually. Very much so. All my sacred enjoyment of spiritual things, the nearness of the Lord and that heavenly peace all seemed to go. Of course, there was no companionship spiritually, there was no ministry, and there was no difference made between Sunday and any other day. It was a very bleak time with me spiritually, but I vividly remember one Sunday evening after landing at Archangel I went into a Y.M.C.A. and the soldiers were singing that hymn of Newton, "How sweet the name of Jesus sounds in a believer's ear", and I remember how my spirit softened to the sound of that Name, and though I was so desolate spiritually I felt there was still that in my heart which could respond to the sweetness of the name of Jesus Christ. Occasionally I would feel a softening of my spirit especially when I thought of the Lord's people in sanctuaries at home, the ministry, and my desolate state, and my feelings were just like those of Israel in Psalm 137.1, "We wept, when we remembered Zion".

On another occasion he related how he went into a cottage belonging to a poor Russian family and there on the table he recognised a Russian Bible. In spite of the spiritual desolation he had been feeling, his heart was immediately touched by a deep sense of love to the Scriptures. By pointing to the Bible and making suitable signs he managed to convey to the family his feelings for the Word of God, and to his joy it was perfectly evident that these were their feelings too.

Back in Tunbridge Wells a lonely Esther waited anxiously for the post to bring her news from Russia, but the solitary time had not been wasted. The Lord was continuing His work in her soul and on the first pages of her diary for 1919 she wrote:

"Looking unto Jesus"
"Ever, only, all for Thee"

This year I desire to keep a little account of events that happen to us as a family and also of the Lord's dealings with my own soul. I have headed this with a text and a line of a hymn; both of these I have taken for mottoes as they mean so much and comprehend such a lot. If we are looking unto Jesus we cannot possibly want for He will supply all our needs. Then I desire that the line of that sweet hymn by F.R.H.* shall describe my life. I feel to come so far short but God knows that I would do everything in the name of the Lord Jesus. When I am dead and gone I should like the words "Looking unto Jesus" put on my memorial card, if I have one, and also this verse:

"Are thy sins beyond recounting,
Like the sand the ocean laves?
Jesus is of life the fountain,
He unto the utmost saves".   *Kent*

This was made very sweet to me at chapel on 30 June of last year at a time of refreshing and revival in my soul that I shall never forget.

As 1919 began, the war in Europe was virtually over but Stanley was still in Russia and on 19 February Esther wrote:

In the morning had a nice long letter from Stan, poor lad, he is heartily sick of Russia and longing to come home.

Though so perplexing and confusing it is evident that this period in Russia was but a prelude to and a preparation for a period of rich spiritual blessing in which he not only proved, as David did, that "He restoreth my soul" but also found that God had a most blessed purpose for the rest of his life which had been so miraculously preserved.

In his own words we have the record of this critical turning point in his life:

*Frances Ridley Havergal.   19

I was in Russia for twelve months, from the middle of 1918 to the middle of 1919, then I returned home.

Esther also recalls this happy occasion on 15 July:

Three weeks ago today our dear old Stan turned up. He arrived in Scotland a week before and called here on his way to Hailsham. He looks and seems much older but is still the same dear old boy.

At the same time she gives an insight into the national joy at the final end of the war:

On the first Sunday of July the signing of Peace was observed through the country in all the churches and chapels. We had a grand service of praise and thanksgiving at chapel in the morning. Mr. Evans made some appropriate remarks and read several portions; he also read the King's Proclamation and an ancient Collect, very suitable for the occasion. We finished up with the National Anthem. In the afternoon we had another Thanksgiving Service (Sunday School) held in the chapel. Mr. B. Wilmshurst (demobilised) read and prayed and spoke to the children, also my dear Stan gave quite a nice address ......We went to 'Rehoboth' in the evening. Mr. Evans was very nice indeed and the ordinance* afterwards was much enjoyed. It seemed nice to see Stanley sitting down among us again after two years of absence.

Stanley continues his recollection of these deeply significant weeks from July to September 1919:

For some time I was in Scotland with very little to do, for the War was over and we were awaiting discharge, and I had ample opportunity to pursue what was in my mind. Well now, it was there in Scotland that I began to feel the call to the ministry. And it came to pass this way.

When we came back to Scotland the Lord was pleased to revive my spirit again. This was not through any particular means, because although I went from church to church in Irvine, I never heard anything that was of a profitable nature at all. The sermons were dry and the ministers simply read them like essays. There was neither life nor power in them to me, so I used to take my Bible and read that instead. I had plenty of time so I took my Bible and went out on the moors where I could be all alone and read. In that way the Lord returned to me, drawing me back again to Himself, and my old feelings of faith and hope and love revived again. But something else came with it. For one thing, I used to find my mind directed to the Epistles of Paul to Timothy, and as I read those Epistles to Timothy which, as you will know, were very largely bearing on the ministry, it seemed to me as though Paul's directions and admonitions were like a living voice speaking to me in those Scriptures. Such as these – "Preach the Word. Be instant in season and out of season." "Let no man despise thy youth", and Scriptures like that. Others that do not just now occur to me seemed to me like a living voice. I do not exaggerate when I say that it could not have been more so if those epistles had been

* That is, the ordinance of the Lord's Supper.

verbally directed to me instead of Timothy. They were so personal. And that was not all. As I used to read and ponder over the scriptures the precious truths of the Gospel were opened up to my understanding in a way and with an effect I had not felt before. They were not new doctrines to me, but they seemed clothed with a new fulness, and depth, and power, especially such a doctrine as the Trinity. Oh, the fulness and the blessedness and the glory I seemed to see in the Trinity, and the Person and work and atonement and sacrifice of Jesus Christ. These truths seemed opened up to me with a fulness that I had not seen before. This produced in me a strong urge to preach those truths. Indeed, whenever I had any fresh entrance into the doctrines of the Gospel it was sure to have that effect upon my spirit, and I felt that I would be called to preach those things. I think it could be said quite honestly that the substance of my preaching over the past fifty years was shown to me and taught to me when I was all alone in Scotland with nothing but my Bible; no minister, no books, nothing but the Bible and prayer.

So it seemed to me as though the words of Timothy were a call to me to preach, and the opening up of those deep and blessed truths showed me what I was to preach. I was to preach those things. And then there was something else. There was the insistence of this word upon my mind in such a way that I could not but feel that it was from the Lord, "Behold, I have set before thee an open door, and no man can shut it."* If the Lord speaks through any particular word He will give us to appreciate what application that word has to us, and taken in conjunction with the other exercises that I have mentioned, I felt no doubt as to what the purport of that word was. The continual insistence of it on my mind made me feel sure that it was not just an act of memory. I did not just recall it, it was insistent. It spoke to me like this - that although I had been in such a dark and desolate state during the twelve months that I was in Russia, yet the Lord had given me a little strength so that I had never given way to temptation, such temptations as beset a soldier's life and especially in a foreign country, and which the other fellows ran into greedily. The Lord had given me enough strength to resist those temptations, even though I was personally allured to them by others, and that I had never denied His name nor denied my faith, nor that I was a Christian. "Thou hast a little strength,..... and hast not denied my name."* Now then "I have set before thee an open door, and no man can shut it." Which seemed to speak to me this way — that when I was discharged from the Army the Lord would open a door for me into the ministry to preach those things that had been shown to me in Scotland, and that there might be some attempt to shut that door, but that "no man can shut it". All of which came to pass.

Well now, that is one side of the matter, but there was another. Because of my extreme shrinking from publicity and my nervousness, the thought of preaching appalled me, and I felt that I never could face up to it — to the publicity of it and the responsibility of it. It seemed altogether too much, and I tried to quench and smother those urgent feelings in my heart and mind by every consideration I could think of — my youth, my inexperience, the

*Revelation 3.8

solemnity of the ministry, the responsibility of it, and the like. O! I tried to pile it all on to my mind to overcome the urge that I felt with regard to the ministry. And I remember those words of the good old prophets of the Old Testament and how well I understood them myself, "And Moses said unto the Lord, I am not eloquent, neither heretofore, nor since thou hast spoken unto thy servant: but I am slow of speech and of a slow tongue".* And that was very true in my case because I was, and the first time I was asked to speak in public prayer in Rehoboth Chapel I stood up and I was so overcome with embarrassment and confusion that I said something or other and sat down without being able to pray at all. I was so nervous. And I sometimes think when our young men commence to speak in prayer at the prayer meeting, they all do better than I did. I could not pray at all. I stood up, muttered something and sat down, I was so overcome with confusion. "O Lord, I cannot speak", I used to say, "I am not eloquent, I have no tongue to speak". And that word of Jeremiah, "Ah Lord GOD! behold, I cannot speak: for I am a child". And the Lord's answer came as well, "Say not. I am a child: for thou shalt go to all that I shall send thee, and whatsoever I command thee thou shalt speak".**

In my concern I felt this word. "I have set before thee an open door", was capable of proof whether it was from the Lord or not. I felt, "Now I will say nothing whatever about this. I will keep my counsel, because if this word really is from the Lord, He will open a door for me into the ministry without my touching the matter". And I thought, "If I say anything, or give any indication that I am under this exercise, I might be very well asked to preach and then I shall never know whether the Lord opened that door or not". So with these feelings very urgent on my mind and spirit I was discharged from the Army, and I came back to Hailsham to live with my mother.

Esther records this happy day:

Wednesday 10 September. Stan turned up at the evening service on his way home after being demobbed; he came home to supper with me.

Then again, a few days later, there is a very significant entry showing the gracious way in which God encourages and compels his ministers to go forward in the work to which he has called them:

28 September. Mr. Evans was exceedingly nice on the subject of the harvest text, "Lift up your eyes, and look on the fields; for they are white already to harvest".† He spoke particularly upon the need there is for prayer that ministers be raised up. Stan came home to tea. I stayed with Ebb in the evening. I went to 'Hanover' and Stan to 'Rehoboth'. He came back to supper and afterwards we went for a walk when he told me a little about his call to the ministry.

Returning to Stanley's account of these unsettled days just after his

*Exodus 4.10
**Jeremiah 1.6-7.
†John 4.35

return from the army, he describes his thoughts and concerns at that time:

Now by this time I had really made very definite plans about my life. I did not want to go back to Tunbridge Wells, I wanted to live with my mother, for I was exceedingly fond of my mother, and my father had died during the War.* And so I came back to Hailsham to pursue my plans for my life, still hoping that I should be relieved of the burden of the ministry.

I had not been home very long before I had a letter from a certain Mr. Lancelot Vinall of Lewes to say that there was a little chapel at Golden Cross that went by the name of the 'Little Dicker' Chapel. It was an independent chapel, a kind of branch of Jireh Chapel, Lewes. It had been closed during the War and he was reopening it and asking for help with regard to the services, and he wrote to ask me if I would take a Sunday service at this little chapel. Well I thought, "Here it is. Now I do not know this man, I have never heard of him". I had only a very faint knowledge of this chapel, and I knew no one who attended there. I had said nothing to anyone and this letter came along to ask me if I would speak at this chapel.

An interesting sidelight on this period of Stanley's life is given in an extract from a letter by an old friend of his, Mr. R. Saunders:

I remember Stanley worshipping at Hailsham Chapel after the 1914-1918 War. His mother had then been widowed and had bought a property in London Road, Hailsham. He used to attend the service at Market Street and it was our pleasure to accompany the old men of those days who would walk home together, after standing and talking (we listening) near to the railway bridge.

He never spoke of his exercises concerning the ministry but I know that when there was a need at the 'Little Dicker' Chapel for a minister, I was led to suggest his name to a Mr. Vinall who was responsible for supplies and Mr. V. then wrote to Stanley who accepted the call and preached his first sermon at the chapel which Mr. John Grace called 'his little Bethel on the Dicker'.

Returning again to Stanley's account:

Well that brought the matter to a head and I did not really welcome it. I was still hoping that I might be able to live a quiet and private life. So I wrote to Mr. Evans at Tunbridge Wells, who was still my Pastor, and told him that I had had this letter and the purport of it and a little of what my exercises of

*In a sermon preached from Psalm 90.16-17, on 18 December 1966 Mr. Delves commented "O! do be thankful for the prayers of your parents. It is wonderful how the Lord can answer prayers. I had praying parents. My father's prayers were weighty simple, solemn. They influence me now. When I was standing with my brother around his deathbed he said, (and it shows how a doubtful spirit can work even with faith). 'I often prayed for my children but I never thought I should live to see them called by grace as I have done'. My father lived to see that. I am glad that he did. O! what a feeling text this is this morning. 'Let thy work appear unto thy servants, and thy glory unto their children'."

mind had been with regard to the ministry. He wrote back and said that he was not surprised; he expected that I should be called to the ministry and others thought so too, which very much surprised me for I had no idea anyone would ever have had any thoughts about me like that. He also said that if I felt the Lord had opened the door I was on no account to shut it. That put the matter back on to my responsibility, so I prayed and pondered and shrank from it and yet I felt I could not say 'No'. So I wrote to this Mr. Vinall, told him that I was not a minister, that I had never attempted to preach, but I would come over on the Sunday and help with the services and see how the matter went. Well, I was very careful, I was not going to commit myself. I was still longing to pursue my plans for a private life. So I went over on the Sunday, found this little chapel, and spoke in the morning without either much liberty or bondage so far as I remember.* I spoke from the memory of the meditation that I had in Scotland. However, in the evening I spoke from another word** and as soon as I had read the verse at once I felt my heart enlarged, and my mouth opened, and I spoke with much liberty without any mental effort at all. It just simply came flowing into my mind. So I set it forth. Well, after the service was over the few friends, perhaps not more than five or six, gathered round me and asked me when I was coming again, and I said, "O, I do not know, you know I am not a minister, I have only just come over to help today. I am not a minister". I would not commit myself. I still held back from it.

Back in Tunbridge Wells, he had a praying friend for whom that particular Lord's day was full of significance. Her record of events is very brief:

2 November. Stan was to preach at 'Little Dicker' today so I am wanting to hear how he got on.

With great concern about the step he had taken, Stanley records:

Well, a day or two after I went over to Lewes to find this good man to ask him however he came to write to me because I knew nothing whatever of him. Well, he was out, he was away, so I could not see him, and actually, soon after that, he moved away. He was an unmarried man and I have never seen him from that day to this, and I do not suppose for a moment that he is still alive. Anyway I felt, "Not many know much about this". I was still shrinking back from the publicity of the ministry. I simply could not get over it, this dread of publicity, and responsibility. I comforted myself with the thought that perhaps I might not hear any more afterwards and that I might settle down to the life I wanted to live. But there was a shock waiting for me for a few days after that I had a letter come along addressed to : "Mr. S. Delves, Baptist Minister, Hailsham"! O dear, I felt as if everything inside of me turned over, and to think anyone should write to me like that — 'Baptist

*The text was Revelation 21.3 "And I heard a great voice out of heaven saying, Behold, the tabernacle of God is with men, and he will dwell with them, and they shall be his people, and God himself shall be with them, and be their God". See page 144 for notes of this sermon.
**Psalm 46.1 "God is our refuge and strength, a very present help in trouble"

Warbleton

My dear auntie

we still miss
you very much
in the sunday
school. mr
Gardener
gave us a lect
ure on Joseph
with letters to
show his chara
cter.

The first letter Stanley Delves wrote

Intelligent
Loving
Patient
Diligent
Wise
Faithful
Joseph was a
type of Chris
we all likea

it very much.
I like reading
about
Joseph and
Daniel this is
first letter I
have ever
wrote
with love
from Stanley

My dear Christine,

This is not much to give you for your birthday as compared with my affection and thankfulness for you.

You and Rachel have always enriched my heart and life with your affection, and especially since Mummy died you have meant more and more to me.

As I get older I value you increasingly.

So while I wish you many happy returns of your birthday, each one will be another occasion of thankfulness to me that you are still preserved to make my last days happy also with your care and love.

The Lord bless you abundantly

Father

A lovely example of Mr. S. Delves' handwriting, as known to so many.

Minister, Hailsham'! And this letter was from Mr. Littleton. That is to say the aged Pastor's son here at Crowborough. He wrote to say that his father had become incapable of preaching, and would I give them some Sundays here at Crowborough. I am not commending myself in this, mind but that is how I felt about it. I thought, "Crowborough — well there is a Church and a congregation and a Pastor. O! I could never face up to that". My spirit failed in me. So I wrote back to Mr. Littleton and told him that he was mistaken, that I had only gone out to help once in a little chapel and that I really could not consider coming to Crowborough to preach. I felt, there is no going there on the quiet and no one knowing anything about it, so I shut that door. But still that gave me no relief at all. The matter got still more and more heavy on my mind, and all my attempts to make my own way in providence were so frustrated and in such a way that I knew it could not be coincidental. O! how I understood those words in the Revelation 3.7, "He that openeth and no man shutteth; and shutteth, and no man openeth". For I was trying to shut the door He opened, and open the door that He kept shutting, and I could not get away with it. About this time I came back to Tunbridge Wells, back to my old work on the Pantiles with my mind, as John Bunyan says, "very much tumbled up and down" with this matter of preaching. Very much so. The burden got heavier and heavier until I really felt this, that either I must preach or else the Lord must relieve my mind of this burden otherwise I would go out of my mind over it. I felt my mind could not stand the strain that I was in.

At this juncture Mr. Littleton wrote again and asked if I would reconsider his letter and come to Crowborough to preach. Well, that letter I just could not answer. If I attempted to say, "No", I felt I was going against the Lord's leading. If I attempted to say, "Yes", I felt I was committing myself to something I could not really sustain. But in the end it came to this point. I heard a sermon on this text "For I am not ashamed of the Gospel of Christ: for it is the power of God unto salvation to every one that believeth",* and under the influence of that I took the great venture — and it was venture — and I wrote to Mr. Littleton and said I would come over on the week evening, and then the friends would know if they wished to hear me any more, and if they did, well I would see how the matter went. So I came over to the Branch Chapel one evening and spoke and I was immediately asked to come again, so I came on a Sunday — the first time I entered this chapel and everything was pretty depressing, and Mr. Littleton said to me, "Can you come again next Sunday?". So I said, "Yes". Well, they had no ministers, I had no engagements, so I came again the next Sunday and then I think I missed a Sunday or so, then I came again, and so it started off with no hand of mine put to it whatever. And I preached very frequently during that year. This was 1920. I was then 23 years old.

Wednesday 21 January 1920 was the date appointed for Stanley's very first visit to Crowborough and on that momentous occasion he spoke from Psalm 35.3, "Say unto my soul, I am thy salvation". No one at Crowborough has left any comment on this first visit but, once again, Esther's diary yields a significant remark:

*Romans 1.16.

I went to the station to meet Ben and Stanley. The latter had been to Crowboro' to preach. Ben said he got on very well; he counted it a privilege to have been able to go and hear him.

In an interesting letter written in 1950 to one of his members, Mrs. Joyce Relf, Stanley refers to his deep sense of need of the Lord's help and blessing in order to be able to preach at all:

I often wonder that I can preach at all, and if a word was not given in time, I should just have to be silent. But that word has been given and I believe blessed. When I started to preach 30 years ago, a friend directed me to a word, I think it was from Berridge; "Pray for preaching food, and what is needful will be given, and what is given will be blessed". And that is how I have found it.

Only those who have experienced these first steps in the ministry of the Gospel can enter into the intense spiritual concern through which Stanley was passing. Not only do the strain and nervousness of these early days take their toll, but facing new congregations of people who are largely strangers and mostly older than the preacher, is something for which special help from God is needed. The "burden of the word of the Lord" without that special and divine help would be unsupportable, but, powerfully encouraged, he continued and was soon preaching every Sunday and sometimes in the week as well.

The mental strain and turmoil of these days was increased by his concern about Esther, for he had now returned to live in Tunbridge Wells and was frequently in her company. On 11 January 1920 she says:

I felt very miserable and low all day and not very well. I couldn't help worrying a bit about Stan as I really don't know how we stand with regard to each other.

Then on 14 January she says:

We have arrived at the conclusion that it will be better for us to be as brother and sister and nothing more. ....For various reasons he does not see his way clear to marrying at present and I for my part think my place is at home.

How many, in similar circumstances, have found that platonic friendships never were possible where true love has once been felt! Theirs was no exception and the inevitable stresses and strains between two people so truly in love soon proved to them both that they were never meant to be "just friends". A few months resolved the question for them and on 19 July Esther records that they had openly commenced their courtship:

> He seems much happier to have it so and I feel it is better though neither of us are in a position to marry for a long time yet.

The first time that Esther heard Stanley preach was on 25 July 1920, when she records:

> I cycled to Forest Fold with Stanley, he preached twice there, very nice sermons which I much enjoyed and so did the people, I believe. Of course it was a great joy to me to hear my boy preach, but at the same time it was rather a strain to hear him especially for the first time. His text was "That I may know him" (Phil. 3.10). We went to tea with Mr. and Mrs. Killick. In the evening Stan preached at Crowboro' Cross (the Branch Chapel), another very nice sermon from the same text. Then we cycled home and had a little communion together.

So commenced a happy and constantly deepening relationship with Stanley working at Durrants in Tunbridge Wells, preaching at the weekends — often with quite long journeys to take, whilst Esther remained with her parents, helping in her father's business and with Ebb, her crippled brother, whose health caused very great concern.

The sober and serious approach to the ministry which marked the whole of Stanley's life was evident in the earliest days and on 30 December Esther gives an insight into his wholehearted concern to redeem the time:

> I went to Ben and Lucy's to a Christmas party. There were about seventeen of us there and we had a very jolly time. Stanley was invited but he did not go as he hardly felt that a party was the place for him, so he came to fetch me home. We both felt that though such things are alright in themselves, yet there is no true and lasting satisfaction or happiness in them.

It is obvious that these years working in Tunbridge Wells and travelling to preach each Lord's day brought Stanley into close contact with the life and testimony of believers in that area of Sussex. Many lasting friendships were formed — mainly amongst the Particular Baptists of the area but also amongst the diminishing number of Independents who had once had such a strong influence on the religious life of the county. Friendships with such men as the late Mr. Mockford and Mr. Reg. Saunders were amongst many others in a group of spiritually minded men in the Tunbridge Wells area who spent many profitable hours in discussions on a multitude of religious topics. Doubtless included were some of the burning issues which vexed the churches at that time. He once recalled a time in these early days of preaching when he was talking with the late John Kemp, who was then the pastor of the Strict Baptist Church at

Bounds Cross, Biddenden. Questioning whether the law was the believer's rule of life, a point warmly debated in those days, the older man quietly and pointedly asked, "Why, young man, which of the commandments do you feel at liberty to break?" Such were the wise and restraining influences under which this young preacher was nurtured and encouraged, until the time came for him to take his place as a teacher and guide of others.

At this time his love for reading must have been developing, a love which continued right to the end of his life, a love so deep that when he was at last too weak and ill to read himself, his daughter and others would read to him from the old familiar favourite — Bunyan's *Pilgrim's Progress*. On one occasion he spoke of the great influence which the writings of Jonathan Edwards, John Owen, and J.C. Philpot had on him, saying that Jonathan Edwards, writing on *Christian Affections,* had had a profound and beneficial influence on his thinking.

One of his members comments on this aspect of his life saying:

Mr. Delves was an avid but perceptive reader. After the Bible, which was his constant companion, he felt certain books had been formative in their usefulness to him. Edwards on the *Affections* he prized greatly, as also Archbishop Leighton on Peter; one of his first members farmed Broadhurst at Horsted Keynes where Leighton had spent much of his retirement. Referring to Philpot's works, he found them profoundly affecting, more so than almost any other writer, "They seemed to strip me of all my religion", but he found them beneficial, contributing to bringing him to those balanced views for which he was so known and loved. "All Philpot's writings are good" he would say, "but in his *Meditations* he gives us the cream."

These then, were some of the varied influences, trials, and joys which were woven together by the Master of his life in these early months and years leading to the commencement of a pastorate which was to develop and continue for the next fifty-eight years.

4

Serving the Lord

1920-1924

"Ye know, from the first day that I came into Asia, after what manner I have been with you at all seasons, serving the Lord with all humility of mind, and with many tears, and temptations".

Acts 20.18-19.

As the year 1920 proceeded so the health of the aged Pastor at Crowborough deteriorated and Stanley was increasingly involved in the ministry of Forest Fold chapel. He speaks of the developments in that momentous period in his life, which was to see him ultimately settled as Pastor of the Strict and Particular Baptist Chapel at Forest Fold, Crowborough:

At the end of that year Mr. Littleton died and as soon as he passed away, (for he never resigned his office), my good friends Mr. and Mrs. Killick, of such beloved and honoured and lovely memory, said to one another that they thought the Lord had brought me here to be the next Pastor, and it got round amongst the members, indeed it was a general feeling that the Lord had brought me to be the next Pastor. However, by that time I had found considerable acceptance in the ministry amongst the various causes and churches, which was surprising to me, and so I went on for a while, frequently preaching at Crowborough and elsewhere until the time came that I was definitely invited, not actually to be the Pastor, but to preach at Forest Fold for six months regularly.

This seemed to bring a heavier burden on my mind than ever. I felt it was one thing to be a preacher and another thing to be a Pastor; however I could stand before one congregation week after week and year in and year out I could not imagine. I felt I should get dried up in no time. But still, for all that, I felt my affections begin to be rooted in this congregation and in this sanctuary so that, although there were intimations to me that other churches had desires towards me, by that time I had become attached to the people here and especially some of the members of the Church. I did not feel I could refuse this invitation but I made it exceedingly clear that I was not committed to anything beyond the six months; that I could not give them any grounds to believe that I should really become the Pastor. So I began the six months.

Unhappily the church records for this interesting period have been lost so that it is impossible to check the dates of events finally. However, throughout his ministry Stanley kept a meticulous record of all the places in which he preached, with the date and the text preached from, and judging by these records it appears that he commenced this six months of ministry at Crowborough in January 1923 when, on the first Lord's day, 7 January, he preached from I Corinthians 2.2-4, "For I determined not to know any thing among you, save Jesus Christ, and him crucified. And I was with you in weakness, and in fear, and in much trembling. And my speech and my preaching was not with enticing words of man's wisdom, but in demonstration of the Spirit and of power".

Continuing with his own reminiscences of this period, he said:

This was my grave concern - would it prosper? Would the Lord further the matter? Was it of Him? Well, the Lord had seemed to be prospering the Word and during that time before I became the Pastor, I had the privilege of baptising Mr. Peter Pratt who was the first of all the numbers of people that it has been my privilege to baptize. That was on 5 June 1921 and, as probably many of you know, he passed away yesterday morning.*

One elderly member recalled that during this period, as the church was becoming more and more attached to the ministry of this gifted young preacher, the church meeting was announced at which the call to the pastorate was to be considered, whereupon word rapidly spread amongst the members that they must all come to the meeting and be sure to vote for him, or else some other church would give him a call and they might lose him altogether. Such was the measure of acceptance which his ministry had found amongst the churches of the area, and such was the love and attachment that the Forest Fold people already felt towards him.

Another elderly member of the church, Mrs. G. Obbard, recalled her own experience during this period:

I was living at Rusthall at the time of Mr. Littleton's death, and on the Sunday following his funeral, I walked up, with a friend, from Groombridge Station to Forest Fold. We were rather late, so went into the vestry. Although, I am sorry to say, I cannot remember Mr. Delves' text**, yet the sermon made such an impression on my spirit that I said to my friend, "He will be our next pastor". Although we had to wait many months for his answer, yet I felt quite sure in my own mind that the impression I had was from the Lord, and I felt quite convinced the answer would be yes. What a great blessing it has proved to myself, and to so many, many others.

The length of time through which these important decisions were considered is indicated by two brief entries in Esther's diary:

*That was 2 June 1972.
**It was I Thess. 4.14, "For if we believe that Jesus died and rose again, even so them also which sleep in Jesus will God bring with him". This sermon is printed on p. 146.

Tuesday 18 October 1921. Went for a walk with Stan at night and he told me all about his visit to Mr. Hider of Crowboro' last night with respect to his call to the Pastorate there.

Sunday 3 June 1923. At Crowboro' today they have been holding their church meeting to vote about Stan being invited to the Pastorate.

The result of the church meeting was an overwhelming majority in favour of inviting Stanley to the Pastorate. The vote was not unanimous, but it was not this which caused his deepest concern; it was the deep sense of inadequacy which he felt in facing such serious responsibilities. As he said, "I could understand anybody not voting for me; what I couldn't understand is why anyone should".

Returning, then, to his own account of the concerns and exercises of soul which he experienced at this critical juncture:

Six months went by, and then there was an invitation given to me to become the Pastor, and what I went through over that I cannot tell you. I felt an attachment to the people and yet it seemed such a responsibility and my spirit failed. I seemed to go all through all my first tensions about the ministry again in regard to the pastorate. Sometimes I felt enlarged in preaching, sometimes I felt contracted. So the time went on and I was asked to give a reply to this letter calling me to the pastorate here in this church. I wrote back with my usual shrinking spirit, for I was very much of a fearful heart and fearfulness seized me again. I wrote and said that if they must have an answer it would have to be No, but if they would be content for me to wait upon the Lord a little longer then I would continue to seek His guidance and His help. I must say it sometimes surprises me how some ministers can accept pastorates so quickly – almost by return of post – when I think of the months of prayer and exercise of mind and waiting on the Lord I went through over this matter. But it stood well!

Now the time went on and it came to a point where it must be one way or the other. By this time the congregation had increased considerably and there were signs of blessing resting on the Word. I particularly remember one Sunday night after I had been preaching at Crowborough that the congregation gathered around me with such evident affection, and on that Sunday the congregation had been particularly good. When I got back home, for I was not married then and I was still living on the Pantiles, I could not sleep that night; it seemed as though the matter had come to a head. At midnight I got up and I could not seem even to breathe in the room, I was in such tension of mind. I opened the window of my bedroom looking out towards Crowborough and – this was not fanciful! – it seemed to me as though the whole congregation came up before my mind just as I had seen them before me that evening. This word struck my mind – "If I forget thee, O Jerusalem, let my right hand forget her cunning. If I do not remember thee, let my tongue cleave to the roof of my mouth; if I prefer not Jerusalem above my chief joy."* And I felt as though everything in my heart went out to the congregation at Forest Fold and that I could prefer them and their

*Psalm 137. 5-6.

spiritual good and profit and blessing above my chief joy. It seemed to me there would be no joy like it. So the next morning I wrote my letter accepting the pastorate. But my fears came back on my mind. I began like Peter to look away from the Lord and my spirit began to sink. I questioned whether I could ever bear the responsibility of the pastorate! So I never posted the letter and Sunday after Sunday I used to come over here with that letter in my pocket, thinking I would see how the matter would go. Time after time I went back home with it at night still in my pocket. But one Lord's day at the Ordinance, something of that same feeling came back to me again as the members were before me at the Lord's table, and I felt, "Now I must do it. If I do not, all my fears will come again". So after the Ordinance I handed the letter to the senior deacon, Mr Hider, and said to him "Mr. Hider, here is my answer to the church". He said, "I hope it is the right one". He was very favourable to me, mind. I said, "Well, Mr. Hider, time will have to prove if it is the right one". That was nearly fifty years ago! Has time proved that it was the right one? I must leave that to you.

Of this development Esther comments:

17 March 1924. Towards the end of the year (1923), after much exercise and searching of heart, my dear boy was led to accept the Pastorate at Crowborough. He was received into the church at Crowborough by Mr. Evans on the first Sunday in January. In five weeks time, all being well, we expect to get married.

Returning to Stanley's own account:

So I began, and the first Sunday on which I commenced my pastorate I hoped the Lord would set His seal upon it, that I should feel confirmed in what I had done, but that Sunday morning was a time of bondage, and heaviness of spirit. When I got back into the vestry I sat down and said "I've finished before I've begun" — just like that: "I've finished before I've begun".*

Well, that seemed very strange to me at the time. But looking back on it I can see now that there was wisdom in it, for if I had gone through that service as we might say 'with flying colours', it might have made me over-confident and I might have lost my dependence on the Lord, and my sense of need that He would be my Helper.

As time went on the Lord was pleased to bless the word, and one after another came forward and I baptized them. Our dear member Miss Day was the first (6 April 1924), Miss Mary Tippett was the next (1 June 1924), and there was a succession of friends who came forward and testified of the blessing the ministry had been made to their souls.

So began this long and honoured Pastorate surrounded with the fervent prayers of all concerned that it would be an arrangement

---

*His text all that day was Ephesians 3.8 "Unto me, who am less than the least of all saints, is this grace given, that I should preach among the Gentiles the unsearchable riches of Christ".

greatly blessed by the Good Shepherd for the building up of the flock at Forest Fold.

Now during this period there were other very important developments, for on 21 April 1924, Stanley and his beloved Esther were married by Mr. Evans at Rehoboth chapel. This day of happiness crowned their venture of faith so that in spite of Esther's weakness there was now a Pastor's wife to move into Chapel House, Forest Fold, only three months after the Pastorate had been commenced.

At their wedding, Stanley's old playmate, Arthur Miles, was his best man. He said that as Stanley and his wife left the chapel after their marriage, friends were about to throw confetti. The bridegroom strongly objected, saying in his Sussex brogue, "I wint go on". The end of this story, unfortunately, is unknown, but it is assumed that, like most people in the same situation, he did go on!

Much later, in 1934, Esther recalled that happy day:-

It is now nearly ten years since I last wrote in this (diary), ten of the most eventful years of my life and ten of the happiest, though we have had many anxieties.

On Easter Monday 21 April we were married at 'Rehoboth' (Tunbridge Wells) by our loved Pastor, Mr. Evans, amid a great crowd of people outside as well as inside. Our reception was at the Belgrave Rooms, after which we went to Brighton, where we spent a very happy honeymoon with Jessie and Edie (Stanley's brother and his wife). We came back to our new home at Chapel House, Forest Fold, Crowborough, on the Saturday and so our married life began.

Chapel House was to be the only home Esther knew as a wife, a home of many memories both joyful and sad. It was a simple home in which visitors were always welcome, a home of warmth and affection, a home of comfort, a home which seemed to be open house to all the congregation on the Lord's day, and in which friends who were unwell would, in later years, be able to sit and hear the services relayed to the comfortable lounge.

There was one room in the house which was set apart, a room which belonged in a special way to the new Pastor. This was his study where he could sit at his desk or in an easy chair surrounded by his books and papers. Only he could possibly know where everything belonged in what appeared, to the uninitiated, to be not exactly a tidy room. Those who came to know him well, and especially his own family, were well aware that he was strongly averse to any change — even a change in the position of familiar items of furniture in the house was not at all welcomed. His study was a place where he could sit, read, meditate and pray surrounded by the familiar sight of favourite books — a room where nothing need be moved — at least not very often! — a room however from which came a constant stream of letters, usually brief, always orderly and truly gracious. It was here that he would spend many hours in preparation for preaching the word, and where so often the Lord met with him. This 'prophet's chamber' was a special place to him, a Bethel indeed, and to those privileged to visit this room there seemed to be an atmosphere of peace which encouraged prayer and meditation.

Much could be said of the home which the happy couple now occupied. Situated in Withyham parish, it is built immediately in front of Forest Fold chapel, between the chapel and the road. From the windows of the lounge it is possible to watch all who enter and leave the chapel. The whole is set in a beautiful rural area which was once true forest but is now a mixture of woodland and pasture, with the slowly growing country town of Crowborough stretching out its housing like tentacles along the roadside towards the chapel lying about a mile north-west of the crossroads at the centre of the town.

The history of the commencement of the chapel is very unusual.*

A godly man, Mr. George Doggett, a farmer in Withyham, some four miles from Crowborough, would travel the nine miles each Lord's day from his lonely farm to Tunbridge Wells to meet with believers in Grosvenor Road, before Hanover Chapel was built. With an increasing family, the journey soon became a problem and he often longed for a place of worship nearer home. In 1832, while he was concerned about this matter, he had a remarkable dream. He saw Crowborough Forest as a great roaring sea, with ships being tossed up and down in all directions and evidently in great danger. As he gazed on the scene he noticed that from a certain spot there shone the beams of a lighthouse by which the distressed sailors were directed to safety.

The dream made a deep impression on his mind, and he felt that it was an indication that it was the Lord's will for him to seek to establish the preaching of the gospel at the very spot where he had seen the lighthouse in his dream. With the memory of the dream still vivid in his mind, the next day he went to the very place and there he found an old thatched wooden barn with a cowshed adjoining, and a few cottages nearby. With others, he obtained a 21-year lease of the barn, supplied seats, and engaged ministers to preach. The district was most unpromising. The people were mostly charcoal burners and diggers of iron ore. Smuggling, poaching, etc., were prevalent. Some were dangerous characters, and one of the early preachers said he was afraid of them. A document described them as "the very ignorant and heathenish people of Crowborough".

The preaching in the barn was the introduction of the gospel into this benighted area. The power of the Holy Spirit made it effectual to the calling

*From, *The S.B.Chapels of England (Sussex)* by R.F. Chambers.

of sinners from darkness to light, and from the kingdom of Satan unto God. Ten persons were baptized in a pond nearby, and a church formed by Mr. Dickerson of Little Alie Street Chapel, London, in 1844. An entry in the Church book recording this reads : "We would lift up our hearts in thankfulness to the God of all grace for the hallowed influence of His Holy Spirit which He was pleased to pour out upon us on that solemn occasion, and we pray that the union thus formed may be strengthened by the addition of many of the Lord's blood-bought, redeemed souls from time to time, and by sweetly influencing us who are thus united by His Spirit as we have received Christ Jesus the Lord, so also to walk in Him". These gracious desires of those foundation members have been granted all through the 130 years which have followed.

Meanwhile the walls of the barn were reconstructed of stone, and a Sunday School commenced in the cowshed, which also has continued to this day, though with some intermission. When the lease of the barn expired an attempt was made by opponents of the truths preached there to purchase it and close it down. By a remarkable providence they were frustrated, a friend of Mr. Doggett having provided the money to secure it only the day before.

Mr. Jonathan Mose, a member at Hanover Chapel, Tunbridge Wells, was the first Pastor; after 8 years he removed to Birmingham. Mr. John Saxby followed, and after fourteen years passed to his rest. During this period a strong wind destroyed the cowshed, and in its place a wing was added to the Chapel.

Then followed the long, gracious, and useful pastorate of Mr. Ebenezer Littleton. The blessing of the Lord rested much on his ministry. He is still held in the affection and esteem of those who remember him. He reached the Jubilee of his pastorate on 5 July 1918, a time marked by the dark and anxious days of the first World War. A special service on the occasion was held at Forest Fold, when a presentation of a framed testimonial and a purse of money was made to him by Mr. Evans of Tunbridge Wells. Mr. Littleton continued a further 2½ years in increasing weakness, and passed peacefully to his rest on 29 December 1920. During his time the Chapel was entirely reconstructed, and stables with a Sunday School room were built at the rear; and additional preaching-places were established at Motts Mill, and the Branch Chapel, Crowborough Cross, the latter still witnessing the affectionate gathering of the congregation on Sunday evenings and weekdays.

What can be said about the state of the church at Crowborough as the new Pastor faced his increasing responsibilities? There had been a period of difficulty and uncertainty as the aged Pastor, Mr. Littleton, became incapable of caring for the church and though led by at least two capable deacons, there had been the inevitable weaknesses produced by lack of leadership and dependence on an itinerant ministry. Happily this unsettled period was not too long as Stanley began to take more and more services, sixteen Sundays in 1920, twenty in 1921 and 1922, then most of the Sundays in 1923.

It seems that the spirit of the church has always been one of gracious independence and whilst firmly Baptist in its church order and Calvinistic in its beliefs, it was never rigidly aligned with any particular grouping within the churches generally known as 'Strict and Particular Baptist', (i.e. practising strict communion and believing in particular redemption as opposed to the General Baptists who were mostly open communion churches and Arminian in doctrine to a lesser or greater degree.) The fact that the church's name appears on the 'Gospel Standard' list of churches indicates that they had at some period signified their agreement with the articles of faith of that group of churches, but their new Pastor never felt free to be exclusively identified with any denominational grouping, maintaining a position of gracious independence and yet showing a loving concern for all churches with similar beliefs and church order. The new Pastor was a man who could truly be said to be a man of peace, a man who always drew his people away from strife and division, a man who, with the Bible in his hand as the ultimate authority in all matters of belief and practice, sought to guide his people into the green pastures and beside the still waters of Gospel truth and New Testament church order.

5

Labouring
Night and Day
1924-1932

"For ye remember, brethren, our labour and travail: for labouring night and day, because we would not be chargeable unto any of you, we preached unto you the gospel of God".

I Thess. 2.9.

The early years of marriage were not easy for the new Pastor and his wife. They faced the many problems which young couples normally have to contend with, but also had to face the many added responsibilities of caring for a growing congregation. Mr. Delves was still working for Durrants and this meant cycling from Forest Fold to Groombridge every morning to catch the train to Tunbridge Wells, with the same journey every evening. He had become very interested in the grocery trade and it is remembered how in the first Sunday School address that he gave at Forest Fold, he confessed his ambition to have a grocer's shop with "STANLEY DELVES" in large letters on the front, but that he now realised this would never be. The Lord brought him to see most clearly that the work of the ministry in feeding souls was far more important than his ambitious plans for a grocery business.

His young wife could not have found it easy to adjust to the new surroundings. She had never lived in the country and was essentially a business woman rather than a housewife. The change from the bustling life of Tunbridge Wells to the rural peace of Forest Fold was very great, and added to this difficulty were repeated periods of ill health. However, she fully united with her husband in his pastoral concern and in later years often spoke warmly of the way she was welcomed to the chapel house, and of the many kindnesses shown to her at that time as the congregation tried to make the house more convenient for her. It is hard to imagine the difficulties of those days when there was no electricity, gas or mains drainage to chapel or chapel house, and some of the mundane tasks the Pastor shared were chopping wood for the chapel fires and emptying the buckets from the chapel toilets.

With three services on the Sunday, morning and afternoon at Forest Fold, and in the evening at the Branch Chapel in the centre of

Crowborough, a preaching service one evening in the week and a prayer meeting another evening, besides many engagements to preach elsewhere, together with the inevitable and numerous duties of a pastorate, the time was very well filled. Also, in these early days of the pastorate, a week evening service was held in a small chapel at Motts Mill about two and a half miles from Forest Fold, but at length the lease of the building ran out and services continued in the dining room of the nearby Hendall Farm until about 1930. This service meant a regular weekly bicycle ride of two and a half miles each way for the preacher. Yet even so, the family have gained, from their father's reminiscences, the feeling that life in those early days was more leisurely than it is now, and after all his duties there was still time for quiet walks together and sometimes with chapel friends.

It is not known for how long the Pastor continued to work for Durrants in Tunbridge Wells but it cannot have been very long, from which time he became entirely dependent on the ministry for all his financial needs.

The new Pastor was a man of many interests and had begun to keep bees; supported and encouraged by Mr. Hider, his elderly deacon, who from the beginning had been very fond of him. However, the man who was born to preach was not over practical and on one occasion had decided to make some new frames for his bee-hives. As each frame was produced it was used as the pattern for the next until, inevitably, the shape and size became very different to the original and they would not fit into the hive. Another of his deacons, Mr. Killick, happened to come along at the strategic moment and immediately saw the reason for the difficulty, explaining that his Pastor must always stick to the original pattern! The deeper, spiritual lesson of this experience was never forgotten and the words of Hebrews 8.5, "See, saith he, that thou make all things according to the pattern showed to thee in the mount", remained as a constant warning never to depart from the original pattern of the Scriptures given by inspiration of God by following even good and gracious men in their interpretation of Scripture.

On another occasion the same deacon, who was also a head gardener, saw his Pastor pruning his rose bushes and strongly advised him not to be afraid to cut them well back. Another lesson was immediately evident — for strong spiritual growth there is need of much severe pruning as the cutting words of Scripture deal with men's sins and weaknesses, their pride and self-righteousness.

The Pastor also had another hobby; the family kept rabbits and it

Mr & Mrs Jonah Delves and their four sons
(Stanley on extreme left)

Birthplace of Stanley Delves

Stanley Delves in Army uniform

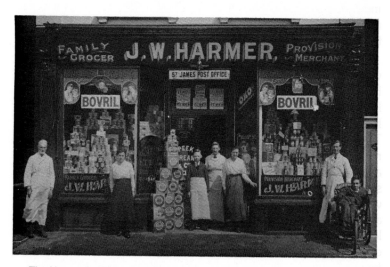

The Harmer's Grocery Business (Esther Caroline on right of doorway)

seemed a strange coincidence that they regularly escaped on Sundays! The young people of the congregation were only too glad to *help* but usually succeeded in chasing them even further away, so that a great deal of time was spent in getting them back in their hutches. In the end the Pastor would laugh at the predicament, while his understanding wife told him he was not nearly firm enough with his young people!

Many pastors have abundant reason to bless God for the gift of a faithful wife and so it was in this case. Only a wife *can* say some of the things which need to be said to a young preacher, so that, right from the beginning of a ministry, annoying and distracting habits can be dealt with. On one occasion the young pastor was chairman for the first time at a local meeting held for the Trinitarian Bible Society. The chairman's remarks grew and multiplied before, at long last, he introduced the visiting speaker. At home afterwards his wife, who had observed the proceedings, said with considerable feeling, "*Who* was the speaker this afternoon?"

Unlike his wife, who was rather the reverse, the Pastor was at his best in the morning. It was not usually very late in the evening when he would retire for the night but he woke early and would spend the first part of the day in communion with his Lord.

During this period the young Pastor's energies were not only directed to his own church at Forest Fold, but he was frequently engaged in preaching, mainly in Strict Baptist chapels over an increasingly wide area. As in his own locality, so in this wider field, his ministry was lovingly received and lifelong bonds of fellowship were formed during this very active period in his life.

A visit to Croydon in 1927 was one which he could never forget. It was in February of that year that his brother Nelson, a Sussex farmer, had been found dead in the most distressing circumstances. Mr. Delves, with his heart almost overwhelmed with sorrow, had to face his first visit to preach at West Street Strict Baptist Chapel, Croydon. The senior deacon, Mr. Hitchcock, seemed somewhat stern when he met the young preacher on his arrival. It was hardly a warm welcome as the deacon had not expected so youthful a minister, and suspected that he would not be acceptable to the large congregation which then met at West Street Chapel. As he entered the pulpit almost every seat was full, indeed visitors often had to wait in the lobby until all the seatholders had arrived before being shown to the empty places. It was generally a prosperous congregation and some families could afford to keep servants. The more radical of the congregation dared to come to chapel by motor car but some of the older members thought this a very worldly, if not sinful, method of transport! It was to this rather formal and very large congregation that the troubled, sad and nervous young minister had to preach. His mind was greatly agitated and discomforted by his cool reception and the thoughts of his brother's death almost distracted him, but the text was a word from God to his own heart, "Be still and know that I am God" Ps. 46.10. Such was the effect of the preaching that the stern-faced deacon was a different man after the service. A bond was established between preacher and people so that a visit which began in such a troubled way was the first of many stretching over a period of fifty years until his last visit in April 1977.

From 1922 to 1940 Mr. George Rose was Pastor at the neighbouring Strict Baptist Chapel in Tamworth Road, Croydon. He also welcomed Mr. Delves into his pulpit, and a deep friendship between the two Pastors continued until Mr. Rose's death in 1965. To the end of his ministry Stanley preached on Good Friday at Tamworth Road and many remember his sermons, usually on the theme of the sufferings of his Saviour.

These visits are typical of many more which the young preacher now began to experience as God extended his usefulness from his native Sussex, until he became known over the whole of the country and was much in demand as a preacher for special services and anniversaries.

Returning to his life and experiences at Forest Fold, it is not easy at such a distance in time to attempt to picture the situation at the chapel in these early days but, for the sake of those who are not familiar with life in such a community, it is needful to attempt at least a sketchy outline. The chapel and chapel house stood in about an acre of land, though at a later date more land was added, making about 1½ acres altogether. This land lies mainly at the north side and to the rear of the chapel where, in the graveyard, the history of chapel families can be read in the loving inscriptions on many stones.

In these early days the congregation would begin to gather as soon as 9.30a.m. for the Sunday School with quite a number having to walk two or three miles to get there. (In later years the Sunday School met from 10.00 to 10.55a.m.) By 11.00a.m. the rest of the congregation had taken their places in the chapel and shortly before that time the Pastor would go up into the pulpit. The deacon, in those days, not only announced the hymns but also read out each verse before it was sung and the singing was led by an organ. It is amusing to read in *A history of Forest Fold Baptist Chapel* published in 1898 by the former Pastor, Mr. Littleton, that the singing had originally been led by a flute, a clarinet, and a bassoon, but at the time of the rebuilding of the chapel in 1897 a valuable organ costing £45 was installed.

After the first hymn, there followed the reading of Scripture by the Pastor who then prayed for about 20 minutes. Then came the second hymn followed by the preaching of the Word from some particular verse of Scripture for about 50 minutes. The service concluded by the singing of another hymn and the closing benediction. Later in Mr. Delves' ministry an extra hymn was introduced between the reading and the prayer to give the ageing Pastor a few minutes' respite. An air of quiet reverence and prayerfulness pervaded the gathering and if the Pastor had felt the blessing of God in preaching he would stay to speak with people as they left. If, however, as sometimes happened, he felt distressed by a lack of liberty in speaking he would hurry away to the chapel house in trouble of soul and pray for a blessing in the afternoon.

Most of the congregation brought a packed lunch with them and would remain in the chapel for their mid-day meal. Cups of tea, made in the vestry, were provided for this meal and nostalgic memories of these cups of tea still remain. The tea was made from water gathered in a large green rainwater tank at the side of the chapel which had its own built-in purifier in the form of a layer of charcoal at the bottom of the tank. There must have been something quite unusual about this tea, as those who remember it can "taste it now!" This habit of remaining for the day at Forest Fold still continues for many and, through the years, has been an opportunity for real communion together, indeed it seems that this habit has played no small part in retaining that sense of close relationship and Christian fellowship which still largely characterises the Forest Fold congregation.

After a second Sunday School at 1.30p.m. a similar pattern of worship followed at 2.30p.m., (this was later altered to 2.15p.m.), when the service would be slightly shorter, as many of the congregation would go either to their homes or to friends for tea and then move on to the Branch Chapel for an evening service at 6.30p.m. (This also was altered later to 6.15p.m.)

After it became known that Mr. Delves had accepted the invitation to Forest Fold the late Mr. John Kemp called him aside one day. "Young man" he said, "I would like a word with you". Expecting some grave advice about the maintenance of doctrine and proper church order he heard these astonishing words — "Young man, if you can manage the heating, the ventilation, and the singing to everyone's satisfaction, you will do very well". Opportunities to show that he could manage, very soon presented themselves! The tradition of lining out the hymns, that is, reading each verse before it is sung, had originated at the time when many of the congregation could not read and few could afford to buy hymnbooks. In the manner of young people in each generation, the youth of Forest Fold then felt that the tradition could well be dispensed with. They therefore got together and wrote a letter to Mr. Delves asking for the hymns to be sung straight through; they each signed their name and, feeling rather important, posted it through the Pastor's letter box the next Sunday morning. When the father of one young lady heard about it, he was very concerned and said severely, "You want to be very careful what you put your hand to!" However, after the service the Pastor quietly gathered the young ones aside and said, "Now I too would like the hymns to be sung straight through, but we do not want to be unkind and grieve our old deacon, Mr. Hider, do we? Wait until he has gone and then we will do as you suggest", and with that most of the young people promptly forgot all about the incident. However, the Pastor had not forgotten and soon after the old deacon passed away in October 1925, the Pastor stood up at the beginning of a service and said, "Now, friends, we will sing the hymn straight through".

It is not wise to estimate spiritual prosperity solely by numbers of church members, nor is it at all correct to think that the number of people baptised represents the total number of those who are brought to spiritual life and conversion. However, since a Baptist Church like Forest Fold consists of baptized believers, such numbers are some indication of the progress of church life, and any pastor, concerned for his flock, longs to see persons "added to the church". As the pastorate commenced the church membership stood at about forty-three but with a total congregation considerably larger. Although baptisms took place during each of the first four years of the pastorate, because of deaths and removals the church membership remained almost static until 1931, when there commenced a steady increase, until in 1936 the number of members was about fifty-seven.

Since the Pastor kept no diary of his own experiences during his many years at Forest Fold, it is only possible to give a very general outline of the continuing work of God at the chapel. Occasional glimpses of the progress of the work are given however in his wife's diaries, and in 1934 she recommenced writing after a gap of ten years. After recalling her wedding day she says:

We have felt very happy among our people here and as time goes on the union seems to get stronger. We have also seen a measure of prosperity in the best things and from time to time members have been added to the church. We have also had many improvements to the house and the chapel and electric light has been installed. My precious husband and I have drawn nearer and nearer to each other as time has gone on, both naturally and spiritually, also I have found his preaching very instructive and very good to my soul many, many times. In 1926 his dear mother was taken home after much suffering; we missed her and still miss her very much. In 1927 his brother Nelson died under very tragic circumstances. In 1928 my dear hubby was ill for several weeks with sciatica and lumbago and went through much suffering, but was restored again. The first year of our married life I was laid aside for several weeks with a bad leg but it got better until 1929 when I was again laid aside for several weeks before the birth of our first little one, Christine Mary. We were very pleased with our little daughter though the first four months of her life were full of anxiety, but after that she thrived and has grown a bonny little maid with an endless capacity for talking.

It was after five and a half years of marriage that the happy news was spread around Forest Fold that the Pastor's wife was to have her first baby, and on 9 September 1929 Christine Mary made her appearance at Chapel House. A child of many, many prayers, she grew to be a comfort to both her parents and eventually a member of her father's own church. It is said that just prior to Christine's birth the parents had both been to a meeting at the Branch Chapel and were about to walk the mile back to Forest Fold when Mr. Delves noticed a friend unexpectedly accompanying his wife. On enquiring as to the reason for the friend's presence he was told that the birth of his first child was imminent, to which he responded, "In that case I will go on ahead and shut the cats up before the excitement starts", to which his wife calmly replied, "There will be no excitement, my dear, unless you make it." But excitement there was for both of them and the deep joy and thanksgiving of parents with their firstborn was enhanced by the joy of their loving friends at the chapel.

These happy times, however, were soon followed by one of the deepest and most distressing of all the many trials Pastor and people had to endure. In their Pastor's own words we are given an insight into the way in which this trial developed with both natural and spiritual aspects combining to bring him to the borders of the grave.

How wonderfully God prepared him for the trial ahead by giving him one of the greatest spiritual blessings he ever had, confirming him in the love of Christ and assuring him of sins forgiven:

> But after a while I came into very great heaviness of spirit again for various reasons. For one thing I found the ministry very heavy on my spirit and for another thing I commenced to read the sermons of Mr. J.C. Philpot! Someone had lent me a book of his sermons and they had an effect on me that no ministry had ever had before or since. But it was a 'pulling to pieces' effect. I felt his sermons so searched me and so weighed me up and so made me feel I was wanting that I fell into a deep concern as to whether I was even right in my own spiritual state after all, and whether my faith and my confidence had not rested too much on the letter of the truth as we say, and not the powerful work of the Holy Ghost in my soul.
>
> Considerations like that pulled me right down and brought me into a great depression of mind. Not that that was unprofitable. I feel that the experience I had, that 'pulling to pieces' experience, has affected the character of my ministry ever since. It has led me to an insistence upon the vital necessity of the Holy Spirit in His teaching in the heart and of the gracious revelation and application of the Gospel with power that I have always insisted on since. I felt it then. I think my ministry would have been of a different character if Mr. J.C. Philpot had not pulled my religion to pieces. However this caused me to feel an extreme regard for that good man Philpot, so much so that I think it is quite true for me to say that I trembled at the word of J.C. Philpot more than I trembled at the word of the living God. So extreme are we apt to get. But we live to learn. I appreciate Mr. Philpot. But still I feel Mr. Philpot's word is only Mr. Philpot's word and it can be quite rightly compared with the Scripture and we are not to call any man master.
>
> My friends, what trouble has been caused all through the Gospel dispensation by an excessive regard for individual men, and especially great men in the ministry. And how much there is in Elihu's word, his inspired word, "Great men are not always wise". Job 32.9. Now we are very apt to think that if a man is a great man in the ministry that he is wise in everything. It does not always follow by any means. Great men are not always wise.
>
> Now all this brought me into a very dark and very burdened state of mind about myself. Other things too gathered on my spirit, until I was brought down so low that I felt I could echo those words of Jeremiah, "My strength and my hope is perished from the Lord".* I remember going out on a business round one morning in this state of mind when the Lord appeared for me wonderfully. I had one of the outstanding experiences of my whole spiritual life. It began like this; that word came to my mind "For as the heaven is high above the earth, so great is his mercy toward them that fear him. As far as the east is from the west, so far hath he removed our transgressions from us".** And, in a way that I cannot exactly describe, my mind and my heart was turned to the Lord Jesus Christ in His sufferings and death for sin and His bearing my sin in His own precious body on the tree.

*Lam. 3.18.
**Ps. 103. 11-12.

The wonderful mystery of Calvary! It seemed unfolded to my mind and my heart wonderfully, and it is true for me to say that it seemed as though the streams of love and mercy and cleansing blood flowed straight from Calvary into my soul filling me with such feelings as I can hardly describe. I remember that morning walking down the High Street, Tunbridge Wells, and it seemed to me as though the traffic in the street and all the noise going on was just a distant rumble, like something on the horizon, and O! I went through that hymn:

> "The wonderful love of his heart,
> Where he hath recorded my name,
> On earth can be known but in part;
> Heaven only can bear the full flame.
> In rivers of sorrow it flowed,
> And flowed in those rivers for me,
> My sins are all drowned in his blood;
> My soul is both happy and free".   *Swain*

I felt every word of it. O! it seemed as though I was full with it. I had never had an experience like that before. It seemed to me as though the power of that love and precious blood of Jesus Christ was such it would have eliminated sin from my very nature. But we live to learn. We live to learn! And it is sad to see what sin can survive in our souls, it really is.

Now that experience was very wonderful to me. I look back on it sometimes and feel that if ever the Lord revealed Himself to me in love and mercy, He did there. I thought "Now I shall be able to preach. Now I shall be able to preach". But a heavy trial was ahead of me, for my life has not been at all an even one. My health had been deteriorating until I got into a very bad state, but the doctor did not seem to take it very seriously. However, my good friend Mr. Edgar Walters of Forest Row, who heard me preach at East Grinstead, took alarm at the condition I was in and, being energetic, he arranged for a doctor to come to Crowborough and have a consultation with my doctor about my condition, which he did, with the result that I was found to be far gone in consumption.* I had to give everything up, preaching and all, and they got me into the sanatorium at Robertsbridge with all good speed, because the doctor told Mr. Walters that night (as Mr. Walters afterwards told me), that the disease had progressed too far for anything to save my life. All that could be done was to get me into a sanatorium. So they got me into Darvill Hall sanatorium. I was then 33 years of age.

In 1934 his wife wrote of this sad time saying:

In the early part of 1930 my dear husband, never very strong, developed consumption and was all the summer away in a sanatorium. He was very ill and to all human appearance would not get better. But the Lord heard the many prayers that went up from all over the country, as well as from our people here, and raised him up again, so that now he is better in health than he was before, though he gets very exhausted and has to take care.

It needs no imagination to enter into the feelings of shock and

*Tuberculosis

sorrow through which his congregation now passed. A sense of bewilderment struck many as they could not understand why one so young and useful should be taken so suddenly from them. One member, who was a child at the time, has recalled the last Lord's day they spent together:

My earliest recollection of Mr. Delves was the Sunday morning before he went into the sanatorium. Although only a child and not fully realising what was taking place, I was conscious of a very great feeling of emotion filling the place, and my own heart. I can still see him, tall, slender and pale, standing just inside the door at the foot of the pulpit steps.

And another member has such a clear memory of the occasion that after all these years the details are recorded:

The last service Mr. Delves took at Forest Fold Chapl before being admitted to the sanatorium at Robertsbridge the next day, is a most vivid memory to me. We sang two hymns given out by Mr. Delves himself. First the hymn of *Cowper* commencing:

"God moves in a mysterious way
His wonders to perform;
He plants his footsteps in the sea,
And rides upon the storm".

The other by *Newton:*

"For a season called to part,
Let us now ourselves commend
To the gracious eye and heart
Of our ever present Friend".

Two other hymns were given out by the deacon — one by *Medley,* commencing:

"Let me, thou sovereign Lord of all,
Low at thy footstool humbly fall;
And while I feel affliction's rod,
Be still and know that thou art God".

And another by *Hart* containing the significant verses —

"Then help me by thy grace to bear
Whate'er thou send to purge my dross;
If in his crown I hope to share,
Why should I grudge to bear his cross?

Though thou severely with me deal,
Still will I in thy mercy trust;
Accomplish in me all thy will;
Only remember I am dust".

The lesson was Isaiah 38 and then Mr. Delves spoke a few words from I Thess. 5.17, "Pray without ceasing". I do not think many of those present thought he would preach again. It was a very sad service and there were very few dry eyes.

Another elderly member recalled her experience at that time:-

When Mr. Delves had been our pastor for a few years, there came a very sad Sunday when he came into the chapel to say goodbye, before entering hospital with T.B. We were all greatly distressed, not knowing whether we should ever see his face again. After the afternoon service I hurried home before the others, and on going to my bedroom I opened the large Bible almost at random, I was in such trouble. I looked down at the page and the very first words I saw were these, "This sickness is not unto death, but for the glory of God".* O! what a change in my feeling! for I felt convinced it was from the Lord, and felt from that time that he would be restored to us, which in a comparatively short time was the case. How true it has proved — that it was for the Lord's glory.

So many of the congregation feared that their young pastor would not make "old bones", as they said, but there was given to them a tremendous spirit of supplicating prayer for his recovery. The prayer meetings held at that time left an indelible mark on the memory of those present and in God's wonderful grace, their prayers were eventually answered.

Returning to his own account of these dark days, he records that:

In the sanatorium there was a long open ward with cubicles, two patients in each cubicle. There was a dispensary in the middle of the ward with two single cubicles each side of it, and into one of those single cubicles I was put, without realising, of course, that being single cubicles that was where patients were put to die, because they did not like a patient to die in a double cubicle with another patient. Actually I saw the patient on my right, on the other side of the dispensary, carried out dead; the patient on the other side of me I saw taken home to die.

Now when I found myself facing death I was exceedingly tried about my spiritual state, and I sank down again. But the Lord appeared for me with this word, "Thou wilt keep him in perfect peace, whose mind is stayed on thee: because he trusteth in thee. Trust ye in the LORD for ever: for in the LORD JEHOVAH is everlasting strength".** And, as I have said sometimes, that word was like a gracious and strong hand reaching down to me where I was, in a low state of body and a low state of mind, lifting me out of it, and putting me again on the one Foundation. And I think I said to my wife "I do not think I shall recover, but I feel sure I shall never sink so low again", and I never did. But for four months in the sanatorium I got first better and then worse until I wrote to our deacons and advised them to call the members of the Church together and accept my resignation, because I felt I should never be anything but an invalid. There seemed no prospect of anything else either. So the deacons wrote to the superintendent of the sanatorium to ask him his opinion about my health, and he gave them his opinion, that the disease was very insidious, had been coming on for a long

*John 11.4
**Is. 26. 3-4

time, and in his opinion I would never be strong.

Well, after four months I got so down in the sanatorium I felt I must come home, and the superintendent's last advice to me was this. He said, "If ever you attempt to preach again, you must never preach more than once on a Sunday, and never more than twenty minutes at a time because your health will never stand the strain". He said that the bottom of my right lung was eaten away and I should never stand the strain. Well, doctors do not have the last word, do they? I was checking up this morning* and I think I must have preached around about 12,000 sermons since then, and on an average of forty five minutes, and often three times on a Sunday, to say nothing of all the other speaking and addressing that I have endured. Brethren, what hath God wrought! What hath God wrought! To raise up a poor consumptive from the grave and maintain him through a laborious life for all these years — about forty. What hath God wrought!

Other friends have filled in a little more of the detail of those days in the sanatorium and one records that:

There was a time when I took Mr. Delves to see Miss Grace Kemp in the same hospital in Robertsbridge. After seeing her in the isolation cubicles, Mr. Delves said "Let us walk back this way", and led me a little way along a path. We paused before a seat, and he said with great feeling, "I remember the first time I managed to walk from the cubicles we have just left to this spot. As I sat on this seat it was as though the Lord said to me 'I have added unto thy days fifteen years'. I thought 'Is it possible I could live fifteen years?' That was just about forty years ago, and the Lord has enabled me all these years for the most part to preach three times on the Lord's day and often in the week. I can only say 'It is the Lord's doing and marvellous in our eyes'."

Another friend remembers a strange incident during his illness with T.B. He was in great distress of mind and thought he would not recover. So much so that when his cousin, Mr. Arthur Miles, visited him he said "All that my child will ever know of her father is his grave". About this time he wrote two letters from the sanatorium, one to his deacons and one to his cousin. The letter to the deacons tendered his resignation. By mistake he put the letters in the wrong envelopes! God, however, over-ruled both events and, as is well known, he was restored to his Pastorate and saw not only his children but his grandchildren grow to adulthood.

In a letter written from the sanatorium on 7 July 1930, he gives another glimpse of his hopes in prospect of returning home:

Through the Lord's goodness to me I am now getting on very nicely, and I quite hope that in time I may be completely restored. The doctor's last examination was very satisfactory and hopeful. I shall be so glad to get back home, even if I am not able to preach, as this is such a spiritually desolate

*2 June 1972.

place here, though naturally I think the treatment has done me much good.

From the end of April to late September in 1930 the Pastor's voice had been silenced by the mysterious hand of Divine Providence. His last full sermon to the people was preached on 24 April from the verse I Cor. 2.5, "That your faith should not stand in the wisdom of men, but in the power of God", and certainly his people were to be shown that their faith was not to rest merely on the words of their Pastor who had been with them "in weakness, and in fear, and in much trembling" (v.3).

After months of prayer, with hopes and fears rising alternately. Forest Fold witnessed the return of their pastor, who gradually regained strength and was able once again to preach to his relieved and comforted people. This return to his own people in the autumn of 1930, however, was in acute weakness and he only preached on five occasions during the rest of that year. The first two sermons on his return so evidently reflected the continuing fear that his sickness was not really cured. On the morning of 21 September he ventured into the pulpit for the first time and spoke from II Cor. 4:16, "For which cause we faint not; but though our outward man perish, yet the inward man is renewed day by day." and on the following Sunday evening his people heard a most pathetic but wonderful testimony as he preached from Psalm 73.26, "My flesh and my heart faileth: but God is the strength of my heart, and my portion for ever". By the grace of God the year concluded with a returning note of hope as his strength gradually increased and he could preach on 7 December from Psalm 73.28, "But it is good for me to draw near to God: I have put my trust in the Lord GOD, that I may declare all thy works", and the new year began with evidence of a new sense of hope for the future and desire for revival as he preached on the opening Lord's day in the year from Habakkuk 3.2, "O LORD, I have heard thy speech, and was afraid: O LORD revive thy work in the midst of the years, in the midst of the years make known; in wrath remember mercy".

What a wonderful answer to this prayer was seen in the record of church membership. The numbers had remained steady at about forty-five for the first seven years of the pastorate, but now there was a quite noticeable increase which continued steadily for the next seven years. Who would have imagined that the first period of real growth in the church would be heralded by the critical illness of their Pastor and his enforced silence for over six months? But God is the sovereign King in His church and will prove the truth of His words to all His children, "For my thoughts are not your thoughts, neither are your ways my ways, saith the LORD". Is. 55.8.

Two letters written some twenty three years after this time of weakness give clear evidence of the hidden purposes of God in allowing such suffering, especially to ministers, when people might naturally feel that God would keep useful servants from such trials. The deepening of understanding and sympathy in the preacher's own heart is a precious gift of God, so that Paul could say "We glory in tribulations also: knowing that tribulation worketh patience; and patience, experience; and experience, hope; And hope maketh not ashamed; because the love of God is shed abroad in our hearts by the Holy Ghost which is given unto us". Rom. 5.3-5.

To Mr. W. Taylor.
18 April 1953

My dear Friend,

This is just a line to send by your good wife to say that we feel very thankful that you have been brought through the operation, though we know that in a case like yours anxiety must persist for some days. We all feel your case so very much indeed on our hearts, and there is, you may be sure, a continual remembrance of you in our affections and our prayers. In my own mind I hoped that an operation might have been avoided, but now that it has been found necessary my feelings turn to pray that, with the Lord's blessing, it may be the means for your permanent relief and recovery. It was a comfort to me to find that the burden of it had been taken from your mind and that you felt a quiet and passive spirit. If you can feel to rest your case of both body and soul on the Lord you will find that He will not fail you whatever may be the issue.

I have, as you will remember, been brought very low and to appearances near the grave, and I sank very low in my feelings; as low, I think, as one could; but I obtained relief from this word, "Thou wilt keep him in perfect peace, whose mind is stayed on thee: because he trusteth in thee. Trust ye in the LORD for ever for in the LORD JEHOVAH is everlasting strength". In any case I have been restored beyond what was thought possible and what has been done in my case can be done in yours, but we cannot foresee the future, and the end must come to us all, there is no avoiding that. However it is our hope and prayer that your days may be lengthened and blessed. I know that your path spiritually has not been as plain and clear as with some, but perhaps the Lord may shine more upon you after this trial, and you may feel to say as many have done "It is good for me that I have been afflicted". In any case it is better for us to look more to Him than to ourselves for there is nothing in and of ourselves but conflict and confusion. I expect to be in Croydon next weekend and will get over to see you all being well.

With my sympathy and affection,

S. Delves.

22 May 1953

My dear Friend,

I feel very sorry that I have not been able to get to see you again. I intended coming on Tuesday of last week as I was at Brixton Anniversary but I understood that you were probably having another operation that day so it seemed unwise to come. As it was I would have come. And now I have so many services on hand and I get so tired between that I cannot do what I would. I have nine preaching services in five days just ahead of me, and not feeling very well.

But that is enough about me. I felt very anxious and burdened about you when I left you the last time. You were so very weak and ill, there seemed nothing I could do but pray constantly for you and your dear wife that you might still be spared to her and your children. Also I wished that I could have been of some comfort to you in a spiritual way, but I believe that you have felt the Lord to be near to relieve and sustain your mind, although for a short time it was otherwise.

The Lord Himself knew what it was to feel forsaken in the most bitter and painful part of His sufferings and though we do not enter into the extent of His sorrow there is a feeling of the nature of it. There are some things we can only learn by experience and often in times of heavy trial. It has been an ordeal to you in body and mind but through it all I feel the Lord's heart has been love to you. I have been relieved and thankful to hear, after your dear ones have returned, that you were gaining a little strength and able to take more nourishment. I quite realise that there is still much need for us constantly to remember you, especially as there may be another operation. Perhaps that may not be necessary. We have been very pleased to have Ruth and Peter over here occasionally, they have been very happy with Rachel, and very good.

I send this note with all my affection and best wishes.

Yours very sincerely,

S. Delves.

6

Rejoicing
and Weeping
1932-1945

"Rejoice with them that do rejoice, and weep with them that weep"
Romans 12.14.

The Pastor's return to his family and to his church was a time of great joy, and together they began to look forward to celebrating the Centenary of the chapel in 1932 for which there were special meetings when the Pastor preached in the evening.

His little daughter Christine was now two years old and in spite of his fears that she would only know his grave, they were together again eagerly looking forward to a further addition to the family and on 1 June 1932 their second daughter, Rachel Esther, was born — a most welcome and wanted addition to the family but an addition who caused havoc to the domestic programme by being too small at birth and then very difficult to feed. Little did the harassed father realise what this daughter would mean to him in later years, but God had His gracious purposes for the future and so the little one began at last to gain weight and strength, eventually becoming a strong and healthy child. Her mother comments very briefly on this event in her diary:

In 1932 our second little girl was born, Rachel Esther; she also was an anxiety at the first but now is growing up healthy and strong. The two dear little ones are a great joy to us.

The period from 1932 to 1939 was one of continuing growth and establishment in both church and congregation at Forest Fold, and by the end of that time the number of members had risen to about sixty. In 1935 his wife could comment:

Last year was a good one for us as a church; we had five new members added at the end of the year. During the year my dear husband had a unanimous call to the pastorate at Brixton Tabernacle, but as he had no leadings in the matter, and as he did not feel he could leave our people at Crowborough at present, he declined the invitation. He has been much engaged in preaching all the year, especially in the summer and autumn at special services.

Another interesting note appears on 17 January for that year:

I forgot to say, in my brief resumé of last year, that we have started a day school in our schoolroom for the benefit of Christine (now five years old) and others about the same age, as all the schools are far away. We have five scholars, the teacher comes for half days at present. The school was commenced last May and the children are getting on very well and like their school and their teacher.

However, the skies over Forest Fold were not always blue and the Pastor had times of temptation as all pastors do, times when there were serious questions about continuing in the same place, times when the enemy encourages doubts and questions and when even small clouds of dissent or difficulty seem to blot out the sun for a while. On Sunday 20 January, the Pastor's wife wrote:

I am still in bed with my bad leg, so not able to go to chapel.....At the church meeting the other night it was mentioned that some thought my husband should not go out to preach so much in the week, as it tires him out for Sundays here. Now this has rather unsettled him again as he feels there is a little dissatisfaction among a few. I hope we may be guided to do what is right, we do not want to leave here if the Lord has a purpose in our staying, and from what some of the members have said to me I feel it would break their hearts if my husband were to go away. But we must wait and watch.

In spite of these unsettling events the year passed without any decision to move away and by 3 January 1937 his wife writes:

Last year was a very good one for us as a church, as we had several additions. (There had been three persons baptized). Today we had very good congregations and my dear husband preached a very appropriate sermon from the words 'Is the Lord among us or not?' Ex. 17.7. At the ordinance he also made unctuous remarks on part of Phil. 3.

Certainly the Pastor had need of the encouragements of 1936 at Crowborough, because during the following year he received a renewed invitation to the pastorate at Brixton Tabernacle. Also, towards the end of 1936, it became evident that the elderly Pastor at Grove Road Baptist Chapel, Eastbourne, Mr. Henry Popham, was very anxious that the young Pastor at Forest Fold should become his successor. The second invitation to the pastorate at Brixton was warm, unanimous and very persuasive but, in the gracious overruling of God, the bonds which held him to his own people were too strong to be broken by the prospect of a possible wider sphere of influence in the metropolis. The reply to the church at Brixton showed that the pillar of fire and cloud still rested over Forest Fold:

To the deacons and members of the Church.

My beloved friends,

In sending my reply to your second invitation to me to become your Pastor, I must explain the reasons for my long delay. I felt very impressed by the consideration that your feelings continued to turn to me, notwithstanding that some years had passed since your first invitation, and that during that time my ministry has continued to be acceptable among you. On my part also, my frequent visits to Brixton have tended to increase my esteem for the cause, and the friends. But at the same time as you communicated with me, I received another invitaton to a pastorate where for many years I have felt a strong attachment, and where there appeared a large sphere of usefulness. There seemed much to be said for my going there if that should be the Lord's will for me.

Together with these conflicting matters there is the further consideration that our people here would be deeply grieved if I were to leave them. During the time that has passed since I declined your previous invitation the Church has been increased more than at any preceding period. I have felt this to be a testimony that it was the right way for me to remain. I have watched most carefully to see if there are signs of my ministry declining here, or of the friends' affection to me waning. But it does not appear to be so.

I trust that you will see how difficult it has been to come to a decision for it is inevitable that I must greatly disappoint two of these three Churches and I love them all. Moreover I have not felt that clear leading from the Lord which would overrule all other considerations entirely.

After anxious and prayerful consideration I feel that I must again decline your most kind and gracious letter of invitation, yet assuring you of my esteem and good wishes for the spiritual welfare of the Church and congregation. I confess to much reluctance in doing so, but find some comfort in the hope that I may be of service to you from time to time if my ministry should still be acceptable and profitable to you.

Yours in the truth and love of the Gospel,

Stanley Delves

1937 must have been a year of many conflicting exercises of mind as the Church at Eastbourne were also very pressing in their invitation. The old Pastor there was one whom Mr Delves greatly respected and Eastbourne was close to the area of his childhood, holding many memories of those happy days of childhood holidays. In March he wrote a letter to Mr. Popham which reveals the mental and spiritual concern felt during this period:

19.3.37

Dear Mr. Popham,

I will reply to your letter at once to explain the position. I intended to call on you on Wednesday but I did not get to Eastbourne till tea time and afterwards there was very little time and I felt that I could not have my mind engaged in this matter immediately before the service. So I asked my cousin, Mr. E. Miles, to explain to you how the matter stood and to give apologies for not calling on you personally. I hope this explanation will remove any impression that I have been discourteous to you as the Pastor.

Now the case stands thus. The Brixton church have renewed their invitation, which is unanimous on the ground that my labours among them since the last invitation have been acceptable to them and signs following confirm them in their feeling that it is the Lord's will for me to go to them as their Pastor. I have of course acknowledged the letter and intimated that I cannot give an immediate decision, but promised to give so important a matter prayerful consideration. You will appreciate the fact that ordinarily I should not have disclosed this to anyone, for it is a private matter of the Church at Brixton, and I trust to you and your people that it will not be generally known. Now I felt in a great difficulty, not only in respect of the ultimate issue, but how to rightly act at the moment, knowing your feelings and intentions which you had told me were shared by the deacons at Grove Road.

Previous to receiving this renewed invitation I had quite felt content to leave the Grove Road question entirely in your hands. If you felt decided to proceed with it, of course it rested with you to bring the matter before the Church. I realised, of course, that it was your considered desire to do so, and that it was not for me to put my hand to it in any way. If the desire of the Church was generally in favour, I should feel the great need of the Lord's gracious direction as to my course in respect of it. In the meantime I have felt the exercise of it almost constantly without seeming to get any farther. On receiving Brixton's letter the position became complicated and I felt very confused. There is nothing concerning a reply within a month. I cannot explain how that point was introduced. I only received the letter a week ago. In the very short time I explained the difficulty to Mr. E.M. not once suggesting that anything should be done without your direction, but that he would state the case to you and the deacons and there I must leave it. It is entirely a matter for you to decide, whether to allow the Brixton matter to be settled first or to take any immediate steps. I know that I feel very greatly tried by these conflicting considerations and not less so because another friend has come forward to join the Church here and others may very likely follow.*

In May he received the formal invitation to Eastbourne but by August the clouds of uncertainty lifted and he could write a definite letter of refusal. Once again the prayers of his loyal and faithful Church at Crowborough had prevailed:

*This copy of the original letter is unfinished.

To the Pastor and Deacons of the Church at Grove Road Chapel, Eastbourne.

My dear Friends,

After very anxious and prayerful consideration I reply to your letter conveying the invitation of the Church to me to succeed the present honoured Pastor upon his retirement. I have felt deeply exercised in the matter. The esteem that I feel for the cause, the liberty I usually feel in the pulpit, and the acceptance given to my ministry among you have given the influence in my mind.

To serve a cause so honoured of God and a people united in the spirit and truth of the gospel as I feel Grove Road to be, would be to me a great privilege and honour. On the other hand, I have every reason to believe that it would be a great sorrow and disappointment to most of our people if I were to leave them. The Lord continues to bless my ministry here and after a number of years there appears no cessation, generally speaking, of the people's attachment to me. We continue to have testimonies of the Lord's favour toward us, and my labours have been more fruitful in additions to the Church during recent years than formerly.

In these circumstances I have felt in a great strait and during the weeks that have passed, I have been waiting for some clear direction to be given me. If I could feel that, other considerations would not, I trust, prevail against it. But I cannot feel satisfied that it is the Lord's will for me to leave my present Pastorate at this time.

To decline the invitation so kindly and graciously expressed in your letter is not easy to me. It is a self-denial. To come to Eastbourne would have many temporal advantages for me and my wife and children. But I have greatly desired that in this solemn matter, my eye might be single to the Lord's honour, and that I might not serve my own interests in the ministry of the gospel. If my coming was not of the Lord, I could not hope that He would be with me in it.

I am sadly conscious that this reply will be a disappointment to many of the friends, some of whom have shown me much kindness. Particularly it grieves me that I cannot accede to the desire of the present Pastor, whose kind interest and concern for my future usefulness has been so evident throughout.

I most sincerely hope that the Lord may provide another who shall be worthy to follow on in the pastoral ministry with which Grove Road has been so signally favoured.

I shall esteem it a privilege to be of any service to you, as at present, as long as you so desire.

With my Christian love and esteem,

Yours in the truth of the gospel,

Stanley Delves

Of these events his wife had but one short comment:

But we feel at present that we cannot make any move from where we believe the Lord has placed us.

One evidence of the love which his people had had for their Pastor was seen during 1937. They realised that with his many journeys to visit his own people and to preach so frequently away from home it would be a great help for him to have a car. Together they collected the sum of £70 and this was presented to him at a Sunday School prize-giving by Mr. H. Dawson, who was then Pastor at Bethersden, Kent. It was some few months after this occasion that the car was purchased as he had difficulty in finding one comfortable enough, which he said was owing to his long legs! Eventually he decided on a Hillman Minx, black of course, and second hand! He had driven on occasions before this, and having a driving licence did not need to take an official test but he was rather nervous of taking his new possession out alone. One of his members, Mr. A. Fermor, (who later became a deacon), who was the chauffeur to a local gentleman, accompanied him on his outings — usually to preach in one of the chapels in Sussex or Kent.

As time moved on towards 1939 there were gathering storm clouds of international tension until finally war had to be declared between Britain and Germany. For everyone it was a time of great concern and a time when, to many, the great truths of the Christian faith seemed particularly relevant. It was sadly a time when most families endured the griefs of separation and in so many cases the grief of losing loved ones in some corner of a foreign field. The rural areas of England were no exception, and Forest Fold has its own roll of honour and its own memories of those sorrowful days.

For a Pastor there was no fear of that official envelope with call-up papers and their notice of conscription, for regular ministers were excused military service so that they could remain at home to comfort and encourage their people.

Crowborough, being south of London, was very well aware of the bombing raids on London, and constantly heard the dismal drone of the German bombers as they flew overhead. But by no means was it just the noise of aircraft that was disturbing; often bombs were dropped as the enemy aircraft jettisoned their load when their planes were damaged by the anti-aircraft guns or fighter planes. Also, there were two quite large army camps in Crowborough, and many of the larger houses were taken over as army billets. The country roads continually rumbled with army tanks and lorries and nearby there were numerous anti-aircraft gun sites and searchlight posts.

Being on the border of Kent, people in the area witnessed much of the "Battle of Britain". During that period the services at Forest Fold were sometimes held with the dogfights going on overhead. The younger part of the congregation (especially the boys) would be quite eager to get out in the break between the services to watch the air battles which were going on overhead. On one occasion during the midday break, a German bomber which had been damaged came over, just skimming the trees. A group of the boys were so certain that it would crash in a large wood beyond the chapel that they decided they would go to search for it — this meant them missing the afternoon Sunday School, but they could not resist the adventure. However, after long searching they found no aircraft, but they did meet an official search party — presumably the Home Guard — who themselves were looking for the same aircraft. They afterwards found that it crashed a few miles away.

Mr. Delves himself was an air raid warden. Wardens were responsible for certain areas in their district and had particular duties to perform, such as making sure there were no visible lights showing from peoples' homes at night time, and that the various rules regarding air raid precautions were carried out. Also, when there was a raid on, which was of course signified by the wailing siren, they had to be on duty and watch out for any such things as fire bombs setting properties alight. When Mr. Delves was away on preaching engagements, Mrs. Delves together with a church member, Mrs. Obbard, who lived just opposite, would stand in for Mr. Delves and undertake his duties.

In the garden of Chapel House there was an underground air raid shelter, which was built for the benefit of the neighbours round about (there being a small group of homes opposite the Chapel which had been built by the local Council). This was in addition to the heavy metal Anderson table shelters which were provided for the individual homes. On one occasion, during a raid, Mrs. Obbard was crossing over the road to enter the shelter when an enemy aircraft came so low overhead 'strafing' the area with cannon fire that she could see the pilot's face as he looked out of the aircraft. One shell fell just near her in the garden, but she was mercifully unharmed. On another occasion the noise of bullets rattled across the Chapel roof during the afternoon service.

It is recalled on one occasion that a visiting minister, who had travelled down from the London area to preach on the Sunday, was expecting quite a restful weekend out in the country away from the fear of bombing and destruction, but he found his 'quiet' weekend a very noisy one and, as he said, "A very frightening one", as all night long he could hear the constant droning of the enemy bombers as they flew overhead, and the noise of the anti-aircraft guns firing. Also of course, there was often the noise of our own bombers as they made their way from the various airfields to attack targets on the continent. It was from such raids that two of Forest Fold's young men never returned. They were cousins, Stanley Obbard and Joseph Obbard. After they were reported missing, there were many, many months of anxious waiting and praying, not knowing whether they had been taken prisoners of war or whether they were injured or killed. In fact, it was not until after the war had ended, and all the prisoners had been returned, that the latter conclusion was really established. Toward the end of the war, the bombers were somewhat superseded by the 'flying bombs' or 'doodlebugs' as they were called. Again, although their target was London, they often fell short and many exploded in the area, making the district more dangerous than ever.

A friend recalls one episode during this war period which showed that the Pastor was a very practical help to his people:

My wife's father owned a large grocery and provision business in Crowborough and during the last war the staff was gradually depleted as one by one they were called up for military service. The difficulties soon became apparent to Mr. Delves, who was fully conversant with this particular business, and so he offered his assistance. How kind and humble his disposition. Nothing too lowly or menial for him to put his hand to, if he could render help or assistance, weighing up the pounds of this and that, serving the customers. So different, so removed from his usual sphere, his pulpit, where we were accustomed to see him, and yet so ready to serve wherever there was the need. How much kinder and more gracious a world if only there were more like him.

Most of the younger men of the Chapel were either away in the forces or away on war work and some of the young ladies too. A few, being farm workers, were exempt and those who were older had local duties connected with the war effort. At one stage in the earlier part of the war, the Pastor's own home was opened to evacuees who had left the more vulnerable areas to come into the comparative safety of the country.

From time to time, soldiers from the nearby camps would come to worship at Forest Fold, and all was done to make them as welcome as possible. It can be remembered that at one time no less than seven were entertained to tea at Chapel House on Sundays and, of course, other friends did what they could in those very difficult days of strict food rationing.

Surrounded by the multiplied griefs of this time of war there was, however, yet another sorrow to be borne, another experience of the mystery of Divine Providence which was part of their cross and part of that experience which would enable the Pastor and his wife to sympathise more fully with their people. Another baby was expected in January 1942 and to the great joy of the household a boy, Stephen John, was born. Again it was evident that the Pastor's wife had a weak child and in spite of the cold weather, the local nurse insisted that she should take the child and care for it herself in view of the mother's weakened condition, for the recurring ill-health of the Pastor's wife had caused great anxiety.

After ten days the crushing blow came and their little boy died. It was the only time one of his daughters ever remembered her father crying, and so intense was his grief that he seldom referred directly to his experience in later years. To a few close friends he confided that this was one of the great sorrows of his life, and on one occasion did mention the experience in preaching. His subject was the Gospel for the Poor,* Luke 4.18, and speaking of the great sympathy of Christ for the broken hearted, he said:

> I remember when I lost my baby boy, which was one of the great sorrows and griefs of my life. My heart was broken over the loss of my little boy, and although it was not that I felt bitter about it, I really was broken. I said to someone that I felt as though I would get up in the middle of the night and go out into the graveyard and bring my little boy back indoors, and he said to me—"O! that was rebellion". I never said any more—I never said any more — that shut me up. Now, I do not believe the Lord Jesus Christ would have said that when my heart was so broken over my little boy. But you see, the other person had never known that grief — he had never known that grief, he could not sympathise, and I could not say another word to him after that. Now, you see, the Lord Jesus Christ knows how to draw poor, broken hearts out, not to shut them up — never a harsh word from His lips to a broken heart!

Because of his own loss he was peculiarly tender towards those experiencing similar sorrows in the loss of children or with handicapped children. Also, this loss raised very acutely the question of the salvation of infants, and on one occasion he confided his

---

*Tape published by the Stanley Delves Trust. Second series No. 3. Part 2. The sermon was originally preached on 14 July 1978.

feelings on the matter to some relatives, saying "I should not say this from the pulpit for fear of being misunderstood, but I believe there is provision in the covenant of grace for all those unable, by reason of their age or immaturity, to understand the nature of the gospel". He was himself specially comforted after the initial shock and grief and given a deep personal persuasion of the eternal safety of his little boy, though no one seems able to remember the precise way in which God mercifully conveyed this assurance to him.

It is possible to trace something of the way in which the Pastor was sustained through this dark valley from the record of sermons preached at the time, doubtless reflecting his concern and fears both for his wife, whose health was so poor, and for the little boy. About the time of his birth he preached a number of times from II Cor. 12.9 "My grace is sufficient for thee: for my strength is made perfect in weakness", and then after the fatal blow had struck he walked alongside another broken hearted father, Job, as he preached from Job 2.10, "What? shall we receive good at the hand of God, and shall we not receive evil?" This was indeed a valley of tears but he could face his own sympathising congregation on 5 February and preach from I Cor. 7.30, "And they that weep, as though they wept not", and then as an amazing proof that the grace of his God was indeed sufficient for him he could speak on 12 February from Psalm 116.7, "Return unto thy rest, O my soul; for the Lord hath dealt bountifully with thee".

The years of national danger and conflict slowly passed until in 1945 the end of the war came — a war during which believers like those at Forest Fold had spent many hours in earnest prayer to God for victory and peace. Through those years the gospel had still to be preached and many were the long delayed journeys which ministers made as they travelled about the country in this work, with the rail service depleted and often disrupted; with no street lights and all car headlights heavily shielded to avoid giving any indication to enemy aircraft of the whereabouts of towns or main roads.

At home the Pastor's wife had many a lonely hour to spend with her two girls to care for and, as she was suffering increasing weakness, there were many trials of faith. In her diary for January 1944 we find:

Seven years since I last wrote: in 1939 the world war broke out and is still raging. In September 1940 four Rye friends evacuated to us and were in our house until June 1943. In January 1942 our dear little Stephen was born but only lived ten days.

61

Again in February 1945 she wrote:

Over a year since I made any entry. The world war is still raging but it looks as though the end of European war is in sight...... I have been laid up from early in December for four or five weeks owing to my old trouble but now have plaster bandages on both legs in order to get about. Rachel had a fall early in January, broke a piece off the tibia, has been in Tunbridge Wells Hospital for an operation and is now home with her leg in plaster-of-paris from thigh to toes, to be kept on for a month.

During last year from middle of June until about September, the flying bombs were a great menace and danger to this part of the country.

Later in 1945, on 2 October, she continued:

Many things have happened since I last wrote. In May the war in Europe came to an end; in August the war with Japan finished; two or three dreadful atomic bombs were dropped on them, then the Russians declared war on them and they soon surrendered......... At present I am keeping in bed as much as possible to try to get my legs better, they have been worse than ever the last few months.... Niece Ruth has received the good news that her fiancé, Wilfred Matthews is alive, after 3½ years of suspense about him.*

So ended a time of unprecedented trouble in England's history, a time when all were involved and when the Church and Pastor at Forest Fold constantly needed a spiritual strength which comes from God Who alone can give that "peace which passeth all understanding".

*Doubtless due to the war.

7

Prosperity
and Adversity

1946-1974

"In the day of prosperity be joyful, but in the day of adversity consider: God also hath set the one over against the other".

Eccl. 7.14.

The years 1946-60 must surely be called the years of reviving at Forest Fold. How wonderful is the sovereign work of the blessed Spirit who, like the wind, "bloweth where it listeth", and how clearly His work is a divine work, often sudden and unexpected. The years of the war had seen a gradual decline in membership at Forest Fold from sixty to fifty-four with many sad losses in the congregation too. But from the end of the war there was a steady increase, so that by 1951 the membership was almost ninety, and that in spite of many deaths amongst the older members. This time of reviving was especially noticeable from 1946-1950, which must have been years of great blessing, and it was on the first Sunday of 1946 that the Pastor reminded his people of the need for a true spiritual reviving when preaching from the Song of Solomon 4.16. "Awake, O north wind; and come, thou south; blow upon my garden, that the spices thereof may flow out. Let my beloved come into his garden, and eat his pleasant fruits." Very powerfully then the Holy Spirit came in answer to this prayer and Forest Fold experienced one of those special "times of refreshing....from the presence of the Lord."

Such periods of prosperity, however, bring added strains into the life of a pastor. Perhaps many church members are unaware of the intense concern which all careful pastors feel about those who apply for membership of the church. Another pastor, John Angell James, once expressed his own concern on this very point: "Hence it is, that some ministers feel it to be the greatest perplexity of all their pastoral avocations, to give answers to persons who come to advise with them on the subject of making a profession. If from suspicion that the hearts of these individuals are not yet right with God, they dissuade them, they may be discouraging those whom they ought to receive and encourage; sending away a babe that ought to be laid in the bosom of the Church; breaking the bruised reed, and quenching the smoking flax: while on the other hand, if they encourage the enquirer to come forward, they may be strengthening the delusion of a self-deceived soul, and become accessory to the ruin of an immortal spirit. Some conscientious men have found and felt this to be the very burden of their lives, and from which there is no way of gaining relief or ease, but by laying down the marks of true conversion, begging the querist to bring his heart to this test, stating what is implied in a Christian profession, and making him responsible for the judgment of his own case, and all its consequences too.''*

The onlookers in a time of blessing see only the joy and share in the rejoicing, but those who carry the care of the church know much of the trials and the bitter opposition of Satan, the great enemy of the true Church. These burdens, together with increasing concern due to his wife's weakness, were doubtless factors which led to another period of illness for the Pastor who was now suffering from a duodenal ulcer.

Reviewing the period in more detail, we find the Pastor's wife writing a typical entry in her diary for 22 July 1947:

I am again in bed, Sir Cecil Wakeley (her medical consultant), to whom I am still going for injections, said I was to have fourteen days in bed so Rachel is staying at home from school to keep house. (Rachel was then fifteen years old). Such a lot has happened since I last wrote. I have been to several Anniversaries with Daddy in the car. Mother and Aunt Annie have stayed with us. We held our Anniversary in June, were crowded at all three services and we provided dinner and tea for all. We have had another soldier's wedding; also the wedding of Ron and Doris Bishop at which there were about one hundred and thirty guests.

Late in 1947 there was an attempt in the locality to get permission for cinemas to be opened on Sundays and at a public meeting the Pastor and others spoke strongly against the proposition, which was happily rejected. This was the year of Princess Elizabeth's wedding to Prince Philip, and on 20 November the diary records:

Princess E's wedding day, we were all able to hear the broadcast of events — a wonderful experience.

It will be difficult for many people today to realise that amongst Christians who were very concerned about the danger of worldliness and the need for believers to be separate from the spirit of the world, the use of wireless had initially been seen as a very serious sign of compromise and lack of spirituality. Sadly, many had become very censorious about those who introduced this modern invention into their homes and it was only the need for immediate news about the

*Extracted from, *The Dangers of Self-Deception.*

war and real fear of a possible invasion that eventually broke down the strong resolve of many never to introduce the 'Devil's Box' into their homes! It is a cause of some amusement and surprise to us now to look back on such attitudes, but the Pastor at Forest Fold was appointed as a "watchman" by his Lord and, without doubt, he showed a deep concern lest this relatively new means of mass communication should become a danger and a spiritual snare to his people. His balanced response to the question prevented this from becoming a divisive issue amongst his people and was typical of his approach to so many of the changes and developments in the world of which Christians are justifiably suspicious. He saw that it was possible to make a careful and Christian use of such a remarkable development in communication without being involved in a sinful abuse of this product of man's ingenuity.

Amongst the many practical ways in which the Pastor assisted his people was in helping with the digging of graves in their own chapel graveyard. This was his labour of love in memory of departed friends as he liked to remove the turf and was very particular about the appearance of a grave. Another typical entry in his wife's diary was for 24 September 1948:

Daddy returned from K and dug grave for Mrs. Akehurst.

Also of interest in 1948 was the comment on 11 October:

Daddy baptized a black man at Brixton.

and on 28 November:

New course of sermons started on eighth chapter of Romans.

New Year's day 1949 marked the completion of twenty-five years in the Pastorate at Forest Fold and there was a very happy gathering at the chapel. Mr. Jacobs presided. Mr. G. Obbard, Mr. Kenward, Mr. Hoad and Mr. S. Fermor all spoke. The Pastor was presented with a cheque for £130 and his wife with a morocco handbag, and as she records:

A sumptuous tea was provided for all.

This was followed on the Sunday 2 January by a special sermon in which the Pastor gave a few reminiscences of the twenty-five years in preaching from 1 Thess. 2.1: "For yourselves, brethren, know our entrance in unto you, that it was not in vain," and many at Forest Fold could now testify to the truth of that verse.

As the year progressed, the thoughts of the Pastor and his wife went back to the first year of married life at Forest Fold, and on 21 April they celebrated their Silver Wedding. The following Saturday they had a small party and Mrs. Delves comments:

23 April. Lovely day. Our S. Wedding party in schoolroom - just the family and the deacons and their wives and a few friends. We had a nice little meeting after tea. Several more presents, cards and 6 telegrams. Daddy went to Croydon in eve.

By 1952 the Pastor's health was giving cause for real concern and his wife comments on 18 March:

Daddy has been very poorly with his D.U. trouble the last few weeks.

She herself was far from well and on 30 July wrote:

I have been in Kings College Hospital for an operation on the veins. Had a fortnight in bed after I got home.

Amidst the growing anxieties of this period, it is hard to repress a smile over the diary for 14 October:

Yesterday and today we have been clearing out the study ready for work to be done on the ceiling and walls, this has thrown Daddy into much confusion of mind and body!

The trouble with the duodenal ulcer continued into 1953, when his wife writes:

22 August. In the morning he visited the Dr. who says he will either have to have an operation or other hospital treatment.
16 September. Daddy had examination at T.W.Hosp. this morn.
18 September. Daddy home again but very poorly.

This pattern continued until October 1955, when he could no longer preach and again his people had the sorrow of being deprived of their pastor's ministry. He notes in his record of engagements after 9 October 1955: "long period of illness", and it was not until 1 January 1956 that the entries resume. His wife commented:

3 December 1955. Daddy has just had six weeks' rest in Crowborough Hospital but does not seem a lot better of the D.U. trouble. He has to have another month's rest at home and then we shall see how he goes on. I am in bed with leg trouble at the moment and Rachel is keeping house and looking after us both.

Significantly, this is the last sad entry in a diary which was never resumed and seems to be in some ways a summary of those constant periods of illness which she patiently suffered for the next eight years. Her husband's trouble with the duodenal ulcer remained one of those thorns in the flesh for some time, but its intensity gradually eased until he was relatively free of pain. He had then to face another minor operation on his hand in January 1957 in the East Grinstead hospital — an operation which not only made a difference to his hand, deformed by Dupuytren's Contraction, but also to his whole appearance, for it was at this time when he found it difficult to shave that he began to grow the beard which distinguished him for the rest of his life.

Those who so well remember the Pastor's wife recall what a wonderful help she was to her husband. Many were the miles she walked to visit the scattered congregation in spite of her legs which became increasingly ulcerated and painful. She was a woman of talent and had some knowledge of French, possessing a Bible in that language. Sometimes when her husband seemed unable to get any light on a text in his meditation, he would ask her to translate it from the French directly and this sometimes gave him the opening he was looking for. Her practical Christianity was known and valued by many beyond the circle of friends at Forest Fold, and a comment from her diary well illustrates what was a typical event in a busy life:

23 April 1946. I took Rachel and five other girls to E.G. (East Grinstead) to visit the Infirmary, they gave sweets and books to all the old women and men.

By the year 1962 Mrs. Delves' condition had so far deteriorated that it was decided she must enter hospital for the amputation of her most seriously affected leg. Everything possible had been done to ease the situation and in Chapel House a hall and bathroom were built downstairs when she could no longer get upstairs, a telephone was installed by her bed and she received every kindness. It was a most distressing case, and despite much prayer and careful medical treatment her condition grew worse. No one will ever know the intensity of her husband's sorrow at this time, as he was gradually brought to the point where he could see that for her "to depart to be with Christ" would be far better than the almost unbearable pain and weakness she was now enduring.

The operation, faced with quiet fortitude, was not to be the way back to health; indeed, her condition continued to deteriorate and at about 8.00 am on 11 August 1963 the Pastor, his family and his flock mourned the loss of one they all so dearly loved. It was the Lord's day, and their Pastor was so amazingly strengthened as to preach in the morning from I Thess. 2.16-17: "Now our Lord Jesus Christ himself, and God, even our Father, which hath loved us, and hath given us everlasting consolation and good hope through grace, comfort your hearts and stablish you in every good word and work." And then just after the funeral he spoke from Rev. 7.17: "For the Lamb which is in the midst of the throne shall feed them, and lead them unto living fountains of waters: and God shall wipe away all tears from their eyes."

Wonderfully sustained through his sorrow, he continued to minister regularly to his own people and to travel extensively during the next two months to places like Shoreham, Watford, London, and Chelmondiston, besides many more local chapels, but at the end of October he had to enter the Kent and Sussex hospital in Tunbridge Wells for a prostatectomy. A successful operation was followed by a period of convalescence at his daughter Christine's home, but his recovery was suddenly interrupted by a most serious attack of virus pneumonia, complicated by a pulmonary embolism. His life hung in the balance as he was admitted to the Redhill General Hospital, where he had to remain until well into 1964.

A great cry of earnest prayer went up to God from Forest Fold and then from all over the country as his many friends pleaded for his recovery. Again, God was very merciful and slowly he was brought back to health, but such a severe illness left its permanent mark and limited his strength for the rest of his days.

Whilst in Redhill hospital he was visited by Mrs. A. Miles, the widow of his cousin Arthur. With laboured breath he said that his testimony could be summed up in a few words:

> "A guilty, weak and helpless worm,
> On thy kind arms I fall;
> Be thou my strength and righteousness,
> My Jesus and my All."
>
> *Watts*

Later in the year he was able to describe his experience over this period in a letter to a fellow minister, Pastor Harold Hoadley, then of Brooke, near Norwich:

1st June 1964

My dear Friends,

I feel ashamed that after your kind and prayerful concern for me I have not written before. I had in fact intended to answer all the letters and enquiries from my many friends but having to rest most of the time between services and other necessary duties I have not kept up with it all.

Christine has told me from time to time that you have phoned her to ask about me, so you will know that I have been very near to the gates of death. It is remarkable that one could be brought through all that came upon me, and it must be ascribed to the Lord's hand upon me in answer to the many prayers offered on my behalf. I am wonderfully recovered and able to preach again though my chest is very weak and breathing sometimes difficult. It may be that some permanent damage may have been caused and I am not young enough to recover from it.

Throughout I have been graciously sustained. In the Tunbridge Wells hospital where I had the operation I was especially favoured with such a sense of the Lord's presence surrounding me as I have not had for many years. Nothing could reach me to distress my mind in the way of temptation, or fear, or care of any kind, and for a time I was so filled with the mercy of God that I could not restrain my emotions. I was glad to be in a single room. Hymn No. 11* expresses my feelings at that time exactly. I lived entirely in that beautiful hymn for a few days. After I left there and went to Christine's I was taken with a much more serious illness and hurried to Redhill hospital on a stretcher where for a time my life hung in the balance. I was too ill to concentrate my mind on anything, except that I felt the truths I had believed and preached would do to die by if I was about to pass away. I walked through the valley of the shadow of death but I feared no evil. The Lord was with me, and in general I felt able to rest in Him.

I have been quite amazed at the concern and affection which has been shown to me from all quarters. I suppose ministers little realize the esteem in which they are held until something occurs to bring it into evidence. One feels so poor in the ministry that it seems to give the feeling that others must feel it poor to them. My own people at Forest Fold could not have been more affectionate to me or more thankful for my restoration to them. I completed, at the end of last year, 40 years of my pastorate. I was then in hospital so that no recognition of it was possible, but a meeting was held last Saturday evening when they showed me a proof of their love to an extent that so surprised me that I cannot seem to grasp it yet.

It is remarkable that my ministry here joined on to my predecessor's because he was unable to preach during the last year of his pastorate and I assisted him frequently, and as soon as he died it was found to be the general desire for me to succeed him. Our combined ministries have covered 97 years.

I hope that you both and all my good friends at Brooke are well. I hear that Mr. Fay is very ill and not expected to recover.

Most heartily I hope the Lord's blessing may abundantly rest upon your ministry at Brooke to the ingathering and building up of many precious souls in the faith of Jesus Christ.

With my love in the truth,

S. Delves

*The hymn in Gadsby's selection by *Stocker* commencing:
"Thy mercy, my God, is the theme of my song
The joy of my heart and the boast of my tongue."

69

In a letter to one of his deacons three years after these experiences, we see again his depth of fellow-feeling and sympathy to those facing hospital treatment:

To Mr. A. Fermor.

14 June 1967

My dear friend and brother,

I feel I must send you this little note as you go into the hospital on Monday. I am sorry that this further treatment is necessary but it may be a good thing that the need for it has been discovered and for it to be treated without delay. We acknowledge the Lord's hand in this and we do pray that with His blessing the means used may be a lasting benefit to you.

I shall continually think of you and pray for you in the hospital as you have done for me when I have been in your case. The Lord has brought me through very serious illnesses as you know, and though we hope that yours may not prove as serious, yet however it may be, He is able to support you in mind and restore you in body as He has done so remarkably in my case.

I hope that you may be kept in quietness and peace of mind. It is something we cannot give ourselves. I have had some of my darkest times in affliction and some of my best. But whatever may be our state of mind we are in the Lord's hands come what may and He is faithful that has promised. It is a great thing to know our foundation and our refuge and, when trouble comes, to feel to rest in Him as being that to us. I hope it is a comfort to you to feel that you have the prayers and affections of us all.

We all love and esteem you..................

During this same year, 1964, the church and congregation had the joy of celebrating the fortieth anniversary of their Pastor's long ministry among them - a ministry which was being richly blessed in the conversion of sinners at that time. His strength seemed remarkably restored and his preaching engagements were all renewed, so that his own people and many congregations far and near were encouraged and refreshed by his ministry.

There followed five years of mature and mellow preaching which made a profound impression on all who heard it. It was a ministry now refined in the fires of deep personal trouble and had about it what can only be described by that indefinable word, 'unction'. His ministry seemed to be loved by all who heard him and it united the various segments of Strict Baptist life in a love to the same truths expressed in such a warm and tender way: and, indeed, his influence spread far beyond denominational limits, as many recognised a special degree of divine anointing and evident spiritual power.

The times of physical weakness, however, were not over and in June 1969 he faced another great crisis in his health and at the

Mr & Mrs Stanley Delves on their wedding day

Cars at Forest Fold Centenary Services 1932,
in the adjacent field.

**Mr & Mrs Stanley Delves with their daughter Christine
(taken late 1931)**

conclusion of the testimony he gave to his church in 1972 he relates the amazing details of his sickness and sudden recovery:

Well now, where shall I end? I think perhaps I had better leave it at this. For I have said enough to show you how I was first brought to the knowledge of the gospel, to believe in Jesus Christ, to feel the sweet and holy peace that His precious blood, believed in and felt, imparts to the soul: how I was baptised, and how the Lord called me into the ministry, and the strains, exercise, helps, comforts, blessings, and usefulness, the Lord has given me in the ministry of His word. And now I am in the evening of my days. I cannot expect — no one can expect — that I shall have many years in front of me now. I would be very thankful not only that the Lord has lengthened my days but that He has given me the strength and help needed to sustain my pastoral ministry and an extensive itinerant ministry as well. It is all entirely due to His gracious favour and purpose towards me. How low I have been brought, and the Lord has lifted me up! What fears have beset me and compassed me around and how the Lord has dispersed them! How near to the grave I have been brought and He has raised me up again from the gates of death!

Because this record will go on the tape perhaps I might mention again my last experience in Richmond Hospital. Friends have often pressed me to write my autobiography and I have never had time to do it or felt inclined to do it, so perhaps this will serve the purpose, and when I am gone if anything is thought worth recording of what I am saying to you now, from the tape — well I must leave it, but I would like to add this because it is the last remarkable experience that I have had.

You know that I was taken ill at Portsmouth.* I went to my daughter's at Surbiton. I was taken worse there and I was hurried off to Richmond Hospital on a stretcher in a very serious condition indeed. And it was thought at the time that it would be my end. It very nearly was. I remember when I was so ill in hospital that our deacons, our brothers Ron and John, came to see me, and I have rather an indistinct recollection of them standing by my bed for I felt so ill, and all I could say to them was that this was my feeling — "Into thine hand I commit my spirit: thou hast redeemed me, O LORD God of truth." For I was hiccupping and, oh violently ill. Anyway, the Lord appeared for me again. I had an operation and it was discovered then that it was not the cancer that was feared. There were other conditions that caused me that deep distress which were relieved. But I had not gone on many days before I was taken with peritonitis and that again brought me down very low. But with the modern methods and injections I was relieved of that.

I thought I should get on better but then it was found I could not swallow, and there was trouble with my throat condition; and I had two minor operations to relieve it — unsuccessfully — until there was nothing for it but another major operation, which would have been the fourth in that hospital. Then it was discovered that my blood was deteriorating and at first that was thought to be leukaemia, but it was discovered to be a failing of the bone marrow to supply certain corpuscles to the blood, and they said there

*This was in June 1969.

was nothing that could be done about it*, that in a younger person it would be fatal, but at my age I might live with it for some time.

Well, there I was again right down. My blood deteriorating, I could not eat anything at all, and only drink a glass of something each day. One night when I was at my lowest ebb my spirit failed again, my old fears beset me and that night when they gave me an injection, and because I knew when I had an injection I should soon be asleep, all I could say was, "Lord, have mercy upon me, for I am desolate and afflicted." I was right down there again. I felt desolate in spirit, afflicted in body, blood deteriorating, major operation ahead. I thought, "If I survive that I shall only be a languid invalid." So I went to sleep after the injection. That night the Lord's healing hand came upon me, and the next morning I was perfectly well. You have heard me say this, that the next morning as soon as I awoke, this lovely word came to me:

> "Though trouble now thy heart appals,
> And deep to deep incessant calls,
> No storm shall injure thee;
> Thy anchor, once in Jesus cast,
> Shall hold thy soul, till thou at last
> Him face to face shalt see." _Kent_

And I sensibly felt the depression lifted from my mind: that my anchor was holding fast and good: that if I died it would be well with me - no fear. But I did not realise that I was healed in body as well as in mind. For the Sister brought me something that the Surgeon wanted me to drink, and I said, "You know, Sister, I cannot drink anything." As soon as I attempted to drink anything, back it was in a minute. She said, "Well, you try." So I tried to drink and I found I could drink without any trouble. I thought, "This seems strange, I cannot feel the obstruction, the trouble." So later on in the day she brought more. I found I could drink that and I began to realise that the trouble was gone. The obstruction was gone. And that evening when they brought the evening meal round I asked if I could have some soup. I found I could take that quite comfortably. By now I was sure that the Lord had healed my body. Well, indeed He had entirely healed my body, and from that time I could eat the meals quite comfortably.

The Surgeon came to see me on the Tuesday evening before she planned this major operation for the Wednesday. She always used to come and see me about seven o'clock before the operation. So when she came, I said, "Miss Waterfall, I am better. I am quite well." She said, "That is very remarkable." So she examined all the plates and X-rays and so on, the blood reports and all the usual details, and she discussed this matter with those that attended her when she came into the ward. "Well, Mr. Delves," she said, "this is most remarkable. You are certainly better and your blood is better, and you can telephone your daughter and say she can come and take you out." Was not that remarkable? That was the evening before a major operation was planned and I have never had any trouble since. And she said, "Your blood is better," and added, which struck me as very

*It was in fact chronic lymphatic leukaemia.

72

remarkable, "This must be an answer to your prayers." I said, "I am sure it is."

Well that was my last experience that I can speak about. The Lord healed me overnight, mind and body, and I have been perfectly well since. What can I say of a God who has been so kind, so gracious, so compassionate, so tender to me? Who has helped me in my weakness, healed me in my sicknesses, forgiven me in my sinfulness and blessed me with the rich blessings of His grace and love in my emptiness. Brethren, no words are capable, no words are capable of expressing the goodness and mercy and love of our God, the Father, Son and Holy Ghost. May His name be forever blessed. Amen.

The amazing suddenness of his recovery is vividly recorded in the two following letters to one of his young people who hoped to be married and, of course, very much wanted her Pastor to take the service:

9 August 1969

My dear R....

As my illness drags on I expect you begin to wonder if I shall be able to conduct your wedding, so I thought I had better explain matters.

I have been, for weeks past, unable to take anything solid without sickness, and it is found that there is a stricture in the food passage. The surgeon has made two attempts to stretch the passage, under anaesthetic of course, but it is not at present known whether this has been successful. I shall see her again next Tuesday and then I may know more. I think she has some other treatment in mind, but if that should fail, it will mean another operation and that would almost certainly prevent me from marrying you on 6 September. I am still holding on to the hope that an operation will be avoided and if once I can begin to take solid food, I shall soon recover. But it may be well for you to have some provisional arrangement with another minister, whoever you would feel to prefer. Mr. D..O.. would be very suitable. I shall be very disappointed indeed if it comes to that. In any case, Mrs. F.. can enter your marriage in our register and issue your certificate. When you get your certificate from the Registrar, I should give it to Mrs. F.. because if, for any reason, it should be mislaid, it would stop your wedding. Please give my kind regards to your mother, P.. and A.. and, of course, to D..

With my best wishes,

Yours very sincerely,

S. Delves.

21 August 1969

My dear R..

I have made a very surprising recovery and hope for the privilege of marrying you and D... Last week the doctor said the only thing was an operation and the surgeon decided to operate as yesterday (Wed.). But I began to recover and found that I could take solid food. When the surgeon saw me on Tuesday evening she was amazed and, though not a religious woman, said this must be an answer to prayer, and I could leave hospital next day. So instead of the operation I came to Christine's; I am letting you know at once about this. I believe you have asked H... to be a standby and I shall be glad for him to help me. I have a lot to make up after all I have been through.

With love to you all.

Your affectionate Pastor,

S. Delves.

Whilst in Richmond Hospital, amongst many visitors was another minister who asked, "Would you like me to read?". "Yes please", he replied, "Will you read Psalm 51? It is just where I am." And to another who visited him when he was so ill that his whole body was being racked by the most violent hiccupping he said with utter quietness and resignation, "I feel that all that is left now is to part with all and prepare myself to meet my Lord."

Even during this time, he was given opportunities to testify to the truth he believed, and when a Roman Catholic nurse commented on his trusting spirit and evident peace of mind, he explained how his faith in Jesus was the secret, and she replied, "I should like to know more about this Jesus."

At this time, there was such widespread unity in prayer for the dear man's recovery, especially at Forest Fold. Not for the first time was there a definite and marked improvement in his condition at the time when his people, and others were blessed with a fervent spirit of prayer for him. Truly it must be said, "Behold, the Lord's hand is not shortened, that it cannot save, neither his ear heavy that it cannot hear." Is. 59.1.

Bunyan's description of the believer's experience is certainly exemplified in the life of this much-tried servant of God:

> "The Christian man is seldom long at ease;
> When one trouble's gone, another doth him seize."

During this time of sickness, and afterward, it was evident that Mr. Delves was finding it increasingly difficult to see. Cataracts were diagnosed and to his great sorrow he gradually became almost blind. With amazing fortitude and determination he travelled all over

England with his white stick, depending on the help of others, so that he could keep his many preaching engagements.

Since the death of his wife he seemed to find added joy and refreshment in his many journeys, especially on his extended tours of Lancashire and the Midlands, when he was so warmly welcomed in the chapels at Nateby, Lymm and Manchester, then at Peterborough, Stamford, Leicester, Coventry, Attleborough, Old Hill and Willenhall. On numerous occasions he would be travelling and preaching every evening for well over a week, which was all the more surprising in view of his condition. Indeed, he became so blind that in the various chapels he visited, the deacons had to read the Scriptures for him, and all his quotations of Scripture were from memory. In God's good providence he was blessed with an excellent memory and once related that when ill and unable to see, he had recited to himself the whole of the Epistle to the Philippians, for which he had a special affection. It was pathetic and heart-moving to see him helped into the pulpit, needing so much assistance, but all such feelings immediately vanished when he began to preach. The memory of those sermons is precious to so many as the peculiar savour and unction of the Spirit was remarkably evident. So often the time slipped by as he spoke, and it seemed that he had only just begun with his subject when the time had gone, and he had to come to an abrupt end, to the surprise and disappointment of the congregation.

During these extended visits it was his special pleasure to meet with younger pastors and share with them some of his wealth of experience and balanced judgment. What encouragement and relief these younger men felt as they realised that their problems were not new, and that one so experienced also found that he faced unsolved questions and new ideas. He had a peculiar ability to draw out younger men into deep discussion of spiritual and theological questions which often ended with a much deepened, more balanced perception of truth, also with the humble conclusion that there was still so much to be discovered. It was somewhat disappointing, not to say daunting, when on later visits, after long discussions on the sad declining state of the churches, he would say "Well, my days are about over and I believe the Lord will help you younger men to face these new difficulties".

This period of increasing blindness affected him deeply. He found the long winter days very dreary, for his wife was gone and his daughter, Rachel, was a very busy professional woman, out for long hours in her arduous and demanding duties in the Social Services of the area. The fact that he could not read was especially distressing and he greatly feared that his ministry would become barren. He once described reading in this way — "Sometimes I try to read the Bible but seem to get no light or help on it, and so I often turn to a good book which stimulates my thoughts and then I can go back to the Bible and read it with renewed pleasure. It is like the old water pump you know; some of them needed water poured down them to prime the pump before you could pump water up again."

In spite of his fears about his ministry his own people testify that it was as fresh as ever. He was greatly helped at this time by friends reading to him, and by tape recordings of sermons. Such was his retentive memory that during this period he was able to conduct a marriage ceremony repeating the service from memory throughout.

Whilst his sight was so poor he was very upset on one occasion when a Crowborough acquaintance commented to another that Mr. Delves had passed her in the street without speaking to her; and we have a glimpse of his kindly spirit when he could not rest until she had been telephoned with his apologies, explaining his predicament.

The pastorate was not without its trials and it is quite amazing what an effect even what might be termed 'minor tremors' can have in the Church. It was at such a time as this when he had to face another perplexing trial. The influence of Pentecostal teaching was increasing in the area, spurred on by the spreading charismatic movement. To the sorrow of the Pastor, Forest Fold was not left unmarked by these events. The Sunday School Superintendent, who had for a number of years been a most useful and energetic leader amongst the Church and congregation as well as the Sunday School and Bible Class, became involved in the 'minor tremors' and misunderstandings. This unsettled state of mind was 'ripe' ground for the seeds of other influences to germinate and gradually it became evident that he was becoming an adherent of the Pentecostal teaching, and after a while he ceased to attend Forest Fold. Although of a strong personality and one who was affectionately regarded by many, God did not allow the Church to be completely divided as has so often happened elsewhere, and the church was deeply thankful to God for the steady and gracious leadership of their Pastor through this difficult period. Besides the family concerned there were a few who left the chapel around this time, but their departure could not be directly attributed to the above event.

On one occasion this same man gave Mr. Delves a lift in his car and began to press him very strongly to allow him to bring their "healer" to his home where they could lay hands on him and miraculously heal him of his blindness. The nearly blind pastor was sorely troubled and experienced the pain that many other believers have had to endure in recent years; the pain of the very forceful accusation that by refusing such an offer he would be resisting the Spirit and throwing away this wonderful opportunity of healing. This greatly disturbed his mind but after much inner conflict he steadfastly refused to walk in this untried path and in due course entered hospital for his cataract operation, only to find, to his great joy, that the specialist was a Christian. He felt the Lord had ordered all things and the operations on both eyes were completely successful. Great was his joy on being able again to see and to read, and he said on one occasion just then, "O, the pleasure of seeing again a child's shining eye, and to see raindrops on the grass."

About this time he had to return to the Kent and Sussex hospital for a second operation on his hand, which was as successful as the first. But then he faced a period of great concern culminating in another period in hospital for investigation for suspected cancer of the throat, which, however, was not confirmed.

These recurring periods of illness forced his church to realise that the Lord was warning them that the time of parting must come. There were an increasing number of visiting ministers who were called in to assist with the afternoon service at Forest Fold or the evening service at the Branch chapel.

In spite of the sadness at seeing their Pastor so much weaker the whole congregation looked forward to 1974 when in May they celebrated the fiftieth anniversary of their Pastor's ministry amongst them. A small booklet was produced to mark this happy occasion, entitled *Unto the Lord,* and extracts from that booklet give us a vivid impression of the spirit of love and harmony that prevailed between Pastor and people after so many years together:

11 May came, and by the good hand of our God upon us, the prayers of so many were answered. Approximately 1100 gathered, and the Lord's presence was truly felt to be among us with that bond of love in the gospel, as so many friends have since intimated. A day indeed to be remembered.

The Pastor welcomed all who gathered, saying:

My beloved friends, to see you all here this morning is quite overwhelming to my spirit, and I feel sure you will not wish me to use a multitude of words and take time assuring you how thankful we feel for the interest and affection which has disposed your hearts to gather here on this day. And so I will say no more than that we most deeply appreciate your presence and feel thankful for your affection, and hope you may feel that this day has been a day that the Lord has blessed.

Another point I want to mention is that there are a number of our ministerial brethren in our assembly this morning, and with my affection to you all, I would gladly have asked each one to speak, but that could not be because of the time; and so it has seemed desirable to confine the speakers this morning and afternoon to our own ministers, who have gone out from our church into the ministry, and our deacons whom we love and esteem. I am sure that none of my brethren in the ministry will feel we have not regarded them in this arrangement.

Another thing I wish to mention, if it is necessary, is that I do hope that through this day a spirit of quietness and solemn and happy thankfulness may pervade this assembly. I regard this as a solemn occasion of worship and praise and thanksgiving to God. The hymns that have been chosen for our worship are expressive of our desire to render praise to the Lord, so that I do hope that all that is done today may be to the Lord's honour and glory. I am conscious — how can I be otherwise? — that I am surrounded and overwhelmed with the affection of so many friends, but I particularly wish that all the honour and praise today shall be to the God of all grace, because it is all due to Him, and most thankfully we would render it to Him. All *affection and esteem* I gratefully receive; *honour and praise* must be entirely to the Lord.

The Pastor's brother, Mr. Jesse Delves of Clapham, then spoke of the gospel ministry, introducing his subject with these significant comments:

The gospel is an everlasting gospel, and although ministers and pastors preach it and pass from this life, it still remains the everlasting gospel of the grace of God, and I would like to speak a word or two upon this point.

First, as relating to *the Divine authority* of the gospel ministry; it is not an institution of man; when the dear Redeemer was here upon earth, before He ascended up into heaven, He sent forth His disciples to go into all the world proclaiming this gospel.

Another point consists in its *continuity*. The gospel ministry has continued nearly 2000 years, and will continue till time shall be no more.

A third point consists in *the subject-matter* of the blessed gospel; the Apostle has affirmed this in a short sentence, "For I determined not to know any thing among you, save Jesus Christ, and him crucified." May we in our ministry keep close to Calvary, for here is the glorious centre and foundation of the gospel ministry.

Others taking part were the deacons, Mr. John Fermor, Mr. John Relf, Mr. Ronald Bishop, Mr. Ernest Constable and Mr. Percy Barker. Also involved in the day's meetings were ministers intimately connected with Forest Fold, Mr. David Obbard, Mr. Henry Godley, Mr. Philip Kinderman and Mr. David Crowter.

In the afternoon meeting, the Pastor preached from Philippians 2.16:

"Holding forth the word of life; that I may rejoice in the day of Christ, that I have not run in vain neither laboured in vain." He spoke of the word of life itself, then of holding it forth and, lastly, of the consequences of holding it forth.

At the close of the services on that memorable day, Mr. Delves was presented with an illuminated address and two comfortable chairs. Replying to this presentation he remarked:

A tribute of a most loving people. John, I remember it was once said by a friend that Stanley Delves can always rise to an occasion, but I can't rise to this and it is no use trying to attempt it. I can only say with all my heart, thank you; throughout these long years I have had the support of faithful men and faithful deacons and I could mention them all, but that's to no point now. But now I have come to the evening of my life and the evening of my ministry; I am surrounded with faithful and affectionate and stable men in office in our Church, and I do not know how to thank God enough for them. They show me every esteem, pay every regard to what I say, consider my feelings in every matter, and what could a pastor have more than that? Men around him and faithful members and friends; a few are still with us who were members in the church when I first came, and another generation is rising up. Well now, perhaps it is not necessary for me to make a speech after what I've been saying today, so very thankfully I accept these gifts from you; and perhaps I might just mention lest there should be any misunderstanding, that I said I did not wish for anything in the nature of a large amount of money to be given to me. I would rather have what was given in that way to be so established as to give benefit to others in years to come; and so I feel quite content about that, and at the same time I appreciate the thought of these kind and useful gifts. So thank you very much.

After a teaset had been given to him for his daughter, Rachel, who had so lovingly cared for him at Chapel house and a nest of coffee tables for Christine and John, he responded:

Thank you very much. It's a very kind thought and with all the feeling that I have today of thankfulness and affection, there is of course that sad feeling at the back of my mind that my dear wife is not here to receive and feel with me the esteem and affection that would have been shown to her so very freely had she been permitted to live to this day. My wife was an ideal Pastor's wife, she really was, and ideal in every way; she was ideal in the sense that she would point out to me anything she thought I wasn't doing right and proper, which is a very good thing in a pastor's wife. She is the best one to do it; but her affection, her usefulness, her quietness and the confidence that the members had in her makes her memory today so fragrant among us. But the Lord has spared to me my two daughters, and my heart and my life is comforted and enriched with their affection; I am very thankful that it was thought of, so that as my wife is not here to receive the esteem so due to her, my two daughters in that sense can receive it and accept it. Thank you very much indeed, John.

From the Sunday School he received a large Axminster rug for use in his study and he then thanked Mr. Constable, a deacon and Sunday School Superintendent, as follows:

'Well, I appreciate this very much and I think the children in our Sunday School know how much I value their affection for me. I have often wondered why children show me the affection that they do, because there is a big gap of age between us, and I thought perhaps I might not be very attractive to children and the girls and boys. I remember I was preaching at Bradford-on-Avon, and when the children came home from their school they came up to see me, and I was so pleased to see their smiling faces. Someone said to me, "Children gather round you like bees round a honeypot", but I never thought they had an attraction to me really, but here and there are children who really show me so much affection. Sometimes they write letters to me, and I always feel exceedingly tender towards them. I think we should be very tender towards the children and young people. Tender in the way we speak to them, and the attitude they see in us in their impressionable days. I think this is very, very nice. It will come into service very nicely indeed and I thank you children, boys and girls and young people of the Sunday School, and the teachers, very much indeed. Thank you very much.'

After tea, numerous friends took the opportunity to visit Forest Fold Chapel, where they were shown around by one of our members. A service of praise and thanksgiving was held on the following Sunday evening 12 May, and a further meeting on Friday 7 June, when the pastor gave an interesting account of the history of Forest Fold as shown on the exhibition boards on 11 May. Pastor was also presented with the Jubilee Record Book, which contained the signatures of approximately 800 of the people who attended.

A lasting memorial to the Pastor was established in connection with these services when a generous collection of £577.57 was added to gifts from local friends to form a fund of nearly £2000. This fund was legally established as the Stanley Delves Trust and still continues, with funds being invested and the proceeds used to assist cases of need such as the Pastor would have approved. Towards the end of his life Mr. Delves gave to the Trustees his approval for making some of his sermons available on cassette tapes, and then since that time they have published a book of sermons entitled *Forest Fold Pulpit*. A fitting memorial to the grace of God in Stanley Delves and a fitting way for his people to show their love in a practical manner for a man who could surely say with Paul, "I sought not yours but you."

8

And Some, Pastors and Teachers.
A Survey of Pastoral Concerns 1924-1978

"And he gave some, apostles; and some, prophets; and some, evangelists; and some, pastors and teachers; for the perfecting of the saints, for the work of the ministry, for the edifying of the body of Christ"

Ephesians 4.11-12.

The most difficult and arduous time in a shepherd's life is lambing time, and the future prosperity of the flock is determined by the number and strength of the lambs born in those often cold and dangerous days of late winter or early spring. So it is with the spiritual shepherd or pastor. His great concern is always to see the flock increased and the growing lambs specially cared for; to see that the older sheep have a right attitude to the lambs, and that the flock is in good health. The perfect example of the Good Shepherd is the pattern which all true pastors strive to follow, and the solemn warnings against the hireling shepherds are a constant reminder that 'soul blood stains deep'! The message of God to Ezekiel is unmistakeably clear: "Son of man, I have made thee a watchman unto the house of Israel: therefore hear the word at my mouth, and give them warning from me. When I say unto the wicked, Thou shalt surely die; and thou givest him not warning nor speakest to warn the wicked from his wicked way, to save his life; the same wicked man shall die in his iniquity, but his blood will I require at thine hand. Yet if thou warn the wicked, and he turn not from his wickedness, nor from his wicked way, he shall die in his iniquity; but thou hast delivered thy soul."

The Pastor at Forest Fold was a man who rejoiced in the privilege conferred on him by his Lord; to preach the Word was his life-long delight and chiefest joy, but he was a man who faced his God-given task with seriousness and a determination to be clear of the solemn responsibility of deceiving souls. His was no ministry of light things, no cry of peace where there was no peace. He preached sin and salvation, the curse and the cross, heaven and hell, but the greatest joy he knew was to preach 'Christ and him crucified'. Through this preaching the Holy Spirit worked with sovereign power, never with any violence or excessive emotionalism; but under the invincible power of God sinners were brought to conviction of sin, to repentance and to faith in the Saviour who was so affectionately commended to them.

The Pastor's concern to see believers gathered into the fellowship of the Church in the scriptural path of baptism is expressed in a simple letter of instruction and encouragement which he once asked his daughter to type out for him. She herself observed his tender concern about the New Testament ordinances, and recalls that he put the observance of baptism very high in importance and viewed the Lord's Supper as a most sacred and solemn occasion. Any slight or disrespect to either of these he would not tolerate and although he seldom preached on baptism as a subject in itself, never putting it in the forefront of his ministry, he included it in a ministry which was balanced and so covered all aspects of revealed gospel truth. It was a cause of poignant sorrow to him when any he had baptized left the truth and turned their backs on what they had professed to believe, even though their number was very small, and he always hoped and prayed that in such sad cases there would be a return to the ways of truth with repentance.

In 1968 he wrote to his daughter saying, "I am writing this from Lymm (Cheshire). I preached in Manchester on Monday, here last night, and am going on to Kirkland to preach this evening and then down to Linslade for the Anniversary on Thursday. At odd times I have been writing the enclosed letter which explains itself...... Could you do me the favour of typing some carbon copies, as many as you can do at one typing".

The following letter is taken directly from one of those carbon copies.

This letter is written as a word of guidance for consideration by friends with regard to Baptism and Church Membership.

Baptism is appointed by direct command of the Lord Jesus Christ for all who by His grace believe in Him and desire to follow Him.

It lays upon all such a solemn responsibility to Jesus Christ to obey that appointment. Also it is in every way desirable that they should profess their faith in that way because it honours Jesus Christ, it builds up the visible church and it tends to the development of spiritual life in the soul which is often much retarded when the ordinances are not attended to.

Baptism is not essential to salvation, but it is joined to that faith which is essential, as it is written "He that believeth and is baptized shall be saved" and what is thus joined together is not to be put asunder.

Baptism and the Lord's Supper are essential to a complete spiritual life and obedience.

But questions may arise which it is the purpose of this letter to answer.

1. Is some special and direct leading of the Holy Spirit necessary?

It is indeed necessary to be guided of the Holy Spirit in all the ways of God, for who is sufficient for these things? The guidance of the Holy Spirit consists chiefly in giving a spiritual understanding to the mind and inclining the heart in the way of truth. Without this, obedience is blind and heartless. This leading many have had, and by not responding to it have quenched the Spirit in that particular. But even so, the way to follow a previous leading is still open.

2. Is a standard or degree of spiritual experience necessary?

In this, one must go entirely by the Scripture. Does the Scripture require it? It is very evident that repentance and faith in Christ were the only necessary conditions for baptism. But where these have been imparted, there will be some experience of the effect of the gospel, usually through the ministry, and this is what the Church desires to hear.

Experiences differ greatly in depth and power and no standard is required.

3. Does the solemn nature and meaning of baptism hinder?

It is one of the most solemn steps one can take and this should be realised. It should deter any from taking it in a light and formal way. But where the spirit is humble and reverent, the nature of the ordinance makes the privilege of walking in it the more sacred to the mind. It should not hinder.

4. Is there a fear of falling afterward and dishonouring the name of Christ?

This is a good fear if it acts rightly in the mind. "Blessed is the man that feareth alway". It acts rightly when it makes one watch and pray and keeps from self-confidence. But if it hinders from obedience to the Lord's appointment it acts wrongly, springs from unbelief and disregards the Lord's ability to hold up our goings in His paths.

5. Does the thought of coming before the Church appear an ordeal?

It all depends how it is viewed. If seen in the light of that Scripture "With the mouth confession is made unto salvation" it is an occasion to make that confession before a company who are glad to hear it. It makes reception into the Church an occasion of spiritual union instead of a mere formality. If it is regarded as an ordeal, it becomes an ordeal which is quite wrong.

The Pastor will be glad to discuss these or any other matters with friends concerned, always remembering that the Scriptures and prayer are the appointed means of guidance to all.

The Pastor's very tender concern about baptism as a command of Jesus Christ to all true believers was demonstrated very clearly on one occasion in 1940. An elderly lady had attended Forest Fold for over 70 years. When twenty-one years old she had made an application for church membership, only to be advised to wait. The effect of this rebuff was so profound that the dear soul had never been able to make a subsequent application. She continued at the chapel and showed the reality of her conversion by a consistent love to the truth, the church, and the ministry. Her Pastor eventually felt that some definite move should be made and contrary to all normal precedents the church was asked to invite this lady to come and give her testimony to them. This story of spiritual trial ended happily with the lady's baptism later that year, followed by eleven more years of devotion to the Lord and to the church.

Another personal testimony shows the care of this shepherd of souls dealing with a young believer struggling with early temptations, fears and embarrassments of making that first confession.

The day the Lord brought me into gospel liberty, I resolved to speak to Mr. Delves in the evening, but for some reason he did not return home immediately after the service, so I sat and waited for him. As the darkness grew around me, so it closed in upon my soul, and all was questioned, so that by the time he came home, I had nothing to say. The only thing I remember of that occasion being the following conversation: "Well, D. what do you really want?" To which I replied, "I want to be more like Him". Gently he replied, "If that is all you feel able to say, I am sure our people would be pleased to hear it!"

A few days later I received the following letter in reply to one in which I had attempted to tell of my soul's experience.

September. 1947

My Dear D.,

I read your letter with very much comfort and satisfaction. I feel that you were able to express your past and present feeling in a clear and acceptable way. Indeed, I felt some instruction as to the nature and working of the grace of God in the soul, imparted to me by it. And that is as it should be: we may learn of another as we listen to the different ways in which the same Holy Spirit brings each one to the same spirit of repentance and faith in our Lord Jesus Christ.

There was everything in your letter that I desired to know. I have passed it on to Mr Jacobs so that I cannot answer the various points. But no answer is required, except to say that it rejoiced my heart to receive it, and I certainly feel it is a testimony for the members of the church to hear.

It was not at all to be wondered at that you felt some opposition of Satan in coming to me on Sunday evening. There is sure to be a conflict in every right way, and much temptation and many alternate conditions and feelings in the mind. You may very likely find it much so at this particular time. Spiritual and gracious feelings are very contrary to the natural state of our hearts, and depend wholly upon the power and influence of the grace of

God, and the Holy Spirit. It is only as we are under that sweet and powerful influence that spiritual things are really felt to be real and precious to us, and our faith and love to them, and to God in them, is in lively exercise. Everything then seems real, true, and clear, as though we could never feel any doubt or question again. But we are not always under the powerful operation of that influence, and then darkness and coldness and indifference and other sinful conditions come over the spirit and make us question all.

Yet with all that there is a maintaining of the principles of faith and love under all these changes which keep us to the ways of God and from time to time we feel a refreshing of our hearts under the word or in some other way. And in all this there is an experimental instruction of our souls, and we have to say, 'O Lord, by these things men live, and in all these things is the life of my spirit'.

With all my heart I wish you all spiritual blessings,

Yours affectionately,

S. Delves.

This kind letter was soon followed by another as this dear friend's wife was constrained to join the church at the same time.

7 October 1947.

Dear D & D.,

I do hope and pray that you both feel confirmed in your mind that you are taking a right step and one which will be honouring to God and good and profitable for you. But that does not mean you will have no conflicts of mind over it, or no changes in your feelings. Whatever is right is sure to be opposed by sin and Satan. You have had some of that experience already. But in quietness and confidence shall be your strength! You join a people who walk together in love and humility and who will receive you with much thankfulness and affection, but in a quiet way. As you know, I am not demonstrative in my feelings, but I have come to feel a deep love to you both and I feel very much encouraged that you find food in our pasture. I look forward to receiving you into the Church in due time.... May the Lord crown all we do in His Name and fear, with His favour in our hearts.

With my love and affection.

S. Delves.

Another striking case of the wonderful and mysterious sovereignty of God, was the conviction and conversion of a very elderly farmer, Mr. Hook. His family went to Forest Fold regularly and often invited him to join them but all to no avail; such things were not for him and he resisted every invitation.

In the garden of the farm there were several fruit trees and over the years Mr Hook had always done the pruning. Although now 87 years old he was one day up an apple tree, pruning, when there in the branches, the Lord began to deal with him. An unmistakable conviction of his deep sin and great need took hold of him and he realised that soon he would have to meet a holy God and a righteous Judge.

In such trouble of soul he now needed no persuasion to go with the family to hear the gospel. The Pastor's ministry completely met his need and the Holy Spirit brought hope to his distressed heart. He found joy and peace in believing. However, during the time of his soul trouble Mr Hook seemed almost senile and incoherent. His Pastor was greatly perplexed by the case and when the poor old man began to ask to be baptized, he feared that his view of baptism was wrong and that he was looking upon baptism as a kind of passport to heaven instead of looking only to Jesus. Frequently the Pastor exhorted him to look alone to the Saviour, until one day when visiting the farm he found the old man in tears and quite inconsolable. Mr. Delves went outside to the daughter and said, "Whatever is the matter with your father, Lily?" "Why" she said, "it is because you will not baptize him". Clearly the matter had to be taken further, and very soon the old man came to tell the church what the Lord had done for his soul.

The following letters to the old man's daughter illustrate the Pastor's careful and loving procedure in this rather unusual case.

12 May 1966.

My dear L.,

I feel so thankful that you feel constrained at last to come forward and to follow the Lord in His appointed way. I am sure that you will have the answer of a good conscience and His blessing in it.

As you know, the procedure is for friends in joining the Church to come before our members and speak of what they have felt in spiritual things and of their leadings in repentance and faith in Jesus Christ.

This is sometimes thought to be rather an ordeal; it was to me, but that is partly because we think that more will be expected than we have to relate. But that is not really so. When Mrs.-- came before the Church recently she quoted that verse very feelingly:

> "A guilty weak and helpless worm,
> On Thy kind arms I fall,
> Be Thou my strength and righteousness,
> My Jesus and my all".

One of the members said afterwards that if she said no more than that it would be enough.

I like to hear the friends say how they are feeling at the present time as well as what their past experience has been.

Also it is a good way for them to let me have a written account of what they feel able to say so that I can remind them at the time if I notice anything is forgotten, and also I can give it to any member who might be prevented from attending the Church meeting.

I am thinking very much about Mr Hook. As you said, it is a pity that his brother has upset his mind about being baptized. I am afraid that if the warm weather goes by he will feel very upset that he has not been baptized when it was suitable and at his age it must be now or never. Of course I cannot decide for him, but I feel that I could baptize him with a comfortable mind, for I am sure he is a right character.

It would be a good thing if we could plan (God willing) the baptizing for the first Sunday of July, The weather would be warmer then, and we can borrow an immersion heater from Rehoboth to save him feeling a chill in the water.

As to him coming before the Church, if you feel that he could do that it would be much better and I would try to help him to say what would be acceptable, but at his age and emotional instability I think the members would receive him on my testimony about him. I should like Mr. John Relf to call and see him as well, if he has not already done so.

I have some hope that you may have a companion to come with you but I cannot say for certain.

I am very thankful that the Lord has appeared for us again for we have had some sad disappointments of recent years.

I think this is all I need say this time.

Please excuse this odd paper,

With my best wishes in every way,

Yours very sincerely,

S. Delves.

Forest Fold 21 June 1966

Dear L,

You and Mr. Hook are constantly on my mind and I do pray that you may feel peace and comfort of mind both in coming before the members next Saturday evening and on the baptizing Sunday. I feel that you will, especially as the matter has been on your mind for so long. But Satan opposes every right step and we are subject to changes in our feelings even when the way is right for us to take, so that you may not always feel as you would like to even now. But you must venture on the Lord and He will not fail nor forsake you. It is not for me to tell you what to say before the Church because that would not be your own testimony, but it may be helpful to you if I give you a little guidance in the matter.

The most important thing is to express your faith and love to Jesus Christ. That is the fundamental principle. Then you could tell us how you first began to be concerned about spiritual things and of any particular times you have had in hearing the preaching or on any other occasions, and of how you came to feel that you must come forward.

I only mention these things because I know that some have been very tried about coming before the church and thought that they would be expected to say more than they felt they could. We are exhorted to give a reason for the hope that is in us and the best reason we can give is that we venture ourselves wholly on Jesus Christ because we believe that He is able to save unto the uttermost.

We are borrowing a heater from Rehoboth Chapel to save Mr. Hook feeling cold in the water and we will make everything as convenient for him as we can considering his great age. But I have no fear but that he will be brought through comfortably.

I expect that G. will bring you up to the church meeting next Saturday but if he is unable we will arrange to come down for you.

I am very much engaged every day this week otherwise I would come down before the meeting so I send this letter instead. If you particularly wish to see me I could perhaps manage it next Friday afternoon. There are others exercised about baptism and I hope this may be a means of their coming forward also, but we want it to be the Lord's work. I believe that will come to G. in time. We can only pray and wait.

With my love to you all,

Yours very sincerely,

S Delves

The baptizing service was conducted without any difficulty and all felt it to be a time of blessing, Old Mr. Hook was full of thankfulness and praise and now, enjoying spiritual peace in believing, he would say with surprise, "All I needed to do was to look to Jesus", which made his pastor think, "How many times I told you that when you were in trouble". Often after hearing the gospel preached he would walk out of the chapel saying, "My last days are my best days, O! that the Lord should have had mercy on *me!*" The Bible was his constant companion, and another friend remembers seeing old Mr. Hook in the kitchen at Hendall Farm, together with another old believer, Mr. Pratt, also in his nineties, sitting in their chairs the whole day, each reading his Bible.

For a further seven years the old sinner, saved by grace, lived to testify to the wonderful mercy of his God, being taken to the 'better country' on 5 January 1973, aged 96, preceded by his old friend Mr. Pratt, who died the previous June aged 91.

☆ ☆ ☆ ☆

Only a Pastor who has watched over souls and prayed constantly for the spiritual blessings of joy and liberty to be given to those in bondage and fear can fully appreciate the intense joy when the blessed Spirit blows as the wind into troubled hearts. That special joy is one of the Pastor's greatest rewards and is so clearly depicted in another letter.

To Mr and Mrs T.

16 February 1955

My dear Friends,

You may have heard from Mr Kenward this morning that he will be coming to see you on Thursday afternoon all being well. It is usual for the Deacons to interview friends before they come before the Church to ascertain a little of their feelings and experience unless they have been members elsewhere and so have already been accepted on their testimony. I thought it would be more convenient to you if Mr Kenward came as he could come during the day when you would be more alone. I am sure you will feel free in speaking to him as he is very gracious and tender in his spirit. I will come before the weekend if nothing prevents. I think I mentioned that there will be a special Church meeting at Forest Fold next Monday to hear the three others who are joining us and there seems no reason why you should not come with them if that will be suitable to you.

I felt so deeply affected by your intimation on Monday evening that I hardly know what to say. If there has been anyone that I have hoped for and prayed for and almost despaired of in this matter, it has been you. When I perceived that the Lord had given you to feel His gracious help and presence in the London Hospital I hoped that if you were brought home again it would have this issue. But when it seemed to pass off and nothing came of it I felt it never would. How true is that line "He tarries oft till men are faint". I felt sure that if you came your dear wife would come with you.

I had occasion to go to Miss D. on Monday about some trees, and I felt it so on my mind to come to you though I should probably have done so in any case. But I seemed to feel there was something waiting for me, but when I found there was, it seemed too good to be true after all the years of exercise in my mind and conflict and trial in yours. I am sure that some at least of our people have felt the same and that much thankfulness will be felt to the Lord that He has appeared for us and for you, and that this will be encouragement to pray and watch for others also.

With my love and affection,

S Delves

Amid the multiplicity of spiritual problems which pastors have to deal with, none are so difficult or delicate as those relating to lack of assurance. The fear that feelings are not sufficiently deep, the question as to whether such feelings are truly spiritual or merely sentimental and the result of a religious or family tradition, are troubles which particularly affect those who have been, from childhood, under the influence of a scriptural and spiritual ministry. The following letter shows a pastor's heart in dealing tenderly with such cases.

Preaching Peace

Forest Fold 25 June 1940

My dear E,

Our conversation the other evening which turned on to spiritual matters has caused me to feel very much about you and what you said to me. I would be glad to be of some personal help to you as well as in the general way of preaching. As far as I remember, the point that fastened on my mind was that you did not feel saved and could not realize for yourself what you desired. That is a very common case, and many draw the conclusion from it that there is something vitally lacking in their religion. Perhaps few comparatively enjoy what they desire to though some are more favoured in that way. It is important to distinguish between principles and feelings. Repentance and faith together with love to the ways and people of God are scriptural and sufficient evidences of a new birth and a spiritual life. The feeling of being saved may be more in the sense of these gracious principles as we seek to walk in them in the fear of God. It may be in your case that you have not so much *felt* to be lost as that you have been brought to see and confess a sinful state and to seek God's forgiveness through Jesus Christ·in respect of it. So in respect of salvation, the important thing is to believe in Jesus Christ with all our heart, which in other words is to be persuaded that He is the Son of God who has suffered in the place of all who believe in Him. That He is the only Saviour and Mediator and as such to seek to come to Him, and to God through Him, for forgiveness and peace.

This believing, if it is a real believing, will always be accompanied with a spirit of desire to know Him in His person, love, and grace and to feel the power and preciousness of His name. Believing is to trust the Lord in everything, as having nothing in ourselves of merit or righteousness. Now when this faith is given, the word of God is that such are fully and freely pardoned and justified from all guilt and condemnation and accepted in Christ. The sense of this is wonderful but all do not realize it as they would. It is the Holy Spirit alone who can so reveal and apply these things. But even if that is in some degree withheld there is a feeding on the gospel in the gracious influence of it on our minds, so that we are not without some experience of the truth especially at times.

It is a mistake to think that spiritual things must be understood and felt all at once. If we are truly being taught of God (and there is no other teaching like it) we come to see and feel things little by little, and what may seem deficient in our case as compared with others will be supplied in God's time and way.

A man whose natural sight was miraculously restored began to see men as trees walking. But the difference between that confused view of things and his previous state of blindness was much greater than between this first dim sight and his perfect vision afterwards. So we should be thankful that we have any sense of the things of God and wait for clearer light and experience. Any who would speak as though you could and should believe and receive Christ just how and when you would, are ignorant of the nature of the Holy Spirit's work in revealing Him and of the exercises of a truly seeking soul.

You made some remark which left the impression that you had some desire to come forward to join us but did not feel to have sufficient ground to do so. I do not wish to press this matter but should be glad to encourage you in it if you felt it on your mind. I think that many who would be right and scriptural characters, hold back far more than they ought. The scripture is the only standard and guide in the matter. If you felt able to give testimony before the Church it would be gladly received, but I know that you would wish to feel a leading in the matter.

I hope that you will receive this letter in the spirit in which it is written and not feel I have taken a liberty.

With my very best wishes.

Yours sincerely,

S Delves

This person was baptized 22 years later at Jireh Chapel, Haywards Heath and later transferred membership to Forest Fold Chapel in January 1967.

Another letter covers much the same ground.

4 February 1936

Dear Mrs W.,

I hope that you will not mind me enclosing a note with my wife's letter. I feel very concerned for you in your present anxieties both naturally and spiritually. Also for your husband and family. You may feel sure of our remembrance of you in our prayers. It is a cloud over you and your home at this time, but there may be blessing in it though at present hidden. We have been so pleased that you have felt led to make Forest Fold your place of worship and we hope and pray that you may be brought through the operation safely and able to come to us again.

I can fully understand how you feel tried and doubtful about your state spiritually. There are many in that case — more than you would think. These are the days when assurance is not so much felt among the people of God though some are more favoured in that way than others. However, assurance is not essential to salvation, neither do doubts and fears shut a soul out of heaven. The essential thing is faith to believe in Jesus Christ and the saving virtue of His righteousness and blood and in that faith to venture our souls implicitly upon Him, foregoing every other hope but in Him alone. We do not need to have any signs of grace in ourselves to thus commit ourselves to Him (although that is in itself a sign of grace), but only to see and feel our sinfulness and utter helplessness to do anything to save ourselves from it. Everyone in that case has the word of God on their side even though they do not feel the express application of it. I was much struck with these lines translated from Martin Luther which I read only last week:

> "Though all my heart should feel condemned,
> For want of some sweet token,
> There is One greater than my heart,
> Whose word cannot be broken.

> I'll trust in God's unchanging word,
> Till soul and body sever,
> For though all things shall pass away,
> His word shall stand for ever".

I fully endorse that, but if the Lord should speak some encouraging word with power in your heart, I know how that would strengthen and comfort you, but His word in the scripture is quite as sure a warrant for you to rest upon so that you venture on Jesus Christ.

With my best wishes,

Yours very sincerely,

S Delves

☆ ☆ ☆ ☆ ☆

An important feature of life at Forest Fold was the weekly prayer meeting in which the men of the church would be asked to pray. This was usually quite an ordeal, especially for those who had but recently joined the church, and the following letter was written to a member who needed encouragement, not only to pray but to pray so as to be heard.

Forest Fold.

Dear G.

I feel I must say how much I felt you were helped to speak in prayer at the Church Meeting, and what a union of heart I felt with you in it. There seemed a very tender and gracious spirit in your prayer which was very impressive to me and others, and I am sure it was acceptable to God through Jesus Christ.

I am sorry that some could not hear you but it is a great thing to speak in public especially at first and no doubt you will be able to make yourself heard as you become more accustomed to speak.

As I think of the way you and L. and your father have been brought in amongst us, I thank God for His goodness and mercy to you and to us in giving you to us as members of our Church. I do pray that others, your daughter among them, may be added to us and that the Church may be kept in the unity of the Spirit and the bond of peace.

With my love.

S. Delves.

In another letter on the subject of public prayer he said:

I am glad that you feel free to write to me about spiritual matters... I doubt if anyone could give you much helpful advice on how to overcome your reserve. In general if you feel it is right for you to pray audibly and you are helped to do so, you will, by being accustomed to the sound of your own voice, gradually gain confidence... no one could have been more shy than I was at first; in fact, when I was called on to pray in Rehoboth, I could not say anything, I was so confused. But if by practice you attained to more freedom of expression you might be tried on the other side even to feel that your ability to pray was more natural than spiritual and more acquired by yourself than imparted by God.

The most important point of all is the need of the Holy Spirit. Without that, all suggestions with regard to prayer, public or otherwise, are worse than useless. With this help you could pray anywhere though it might be with groanings which cannot be uttered. Without it, you could not pray, though you might speak in a very self-controlled and orderly and commendable manner.....

I often feel that my prayers bring few blessings because I do not sufficiently pray "In the Holy Ghost".

☆ ☆ ☆ ☆ ☆

A notable evidence of God's blessing at Forest Fold over the long years of this pastorate was the way in which a succession of gracious men were called and equipped for the public ministry of the word, becoming most acceptable itinerant preachers and, in some cases, pastors. Mr Jacobs began to preach in August 1946 and died in December 1962. Mr Obbard spoke of his call to preach before the church on 3 October 1955, and was subsequently appointed Pastor at Rehoboth Chapel, Tunbridge Wells, on 13 October 1962. Mr. Henry Godley was commended by the church to the work of the ministry on 25 January 1958. and became Pastor at Bodle Street on 16 December 1964. Mr. Philip Kinderman spoke to the church on 9 April 1961, and was called to the pastorate at Mayfield on 26 October 1968. Mr. John Relf was encouraged to preach by the church on 19 October 1964, and Mr. David Crowter on 29 April 1967. Two of these ministers, Mr. D. Obbard and Mr. H. Godley were born again under Mr. Delves' ministry, and the witness of all five of these men was that the Pastor's ministry was of great spiritual help and blessing to them.

The divine call to preach is peculiar and individual and the ultimate proof of its origin is to be seen in its consequent influence and usefulness. Mr. Delves was a man with very high standards in regard to the public ministry, so much so that on one occasion in a time of illness the Doctor questioned him about his attitude to his work of preaching, having realised that no small part of the illness was due to the constant desire to reach a standard in the ministry which was never attained. In answer to the Doctor's questioning he said, "Well, Doctor, I think I know what preaching ought to be".

A man with these standards was not quick to encourage younger men to go forward in the ministry unless he was well persuaded that the call was indeed from God.

The following letter clearly demonstrates this cautious yet tenderly encouraging approach.

April 1952

My dear D.,

I wish that I could feel to have grace and understanding sufficient to write a suitable and helpful letter to you concerning the very solemn matter now exercising your mind. Indeed it is one which must to a great extent rest between your own soul and God. No one is in a position to say what you should or should not do, nor would it be right for you to act upon such advice even though it should come from one in whom you felt confidence.

In entering the ministry, the first step is of the greatest importance because if you do not feel the Lord to be with you in it, and cannot see His hand in opening the door, it will give the enemy an occasion to distress your mind, perhaps for the rest of your days. Besides, you would not wish to take such a step unless you could feel the Lord's guiding and supporting hand.

You may be sure I feel a very tender and anxious sympathy with you, and whatever may be the issue of your present exercise, you will have my heart with you in it.

I would point out one or two considerations which might be helpful to you. It is not wise in such a step as this to act under the immediate influence of a special time of blessing. In respect to the ordinances and one's profession, it is somewhat different, because, as I think I mentioned, that is the appointed path for all believers. When one is under the powerful influence and sense of the love of Christ, the effect often is to stimulate a desire, which in and of itself is a right one, to open one's lips to show forth His praise. But experience has shown that this is not in and of itself a call to the ministry. On the other hand, it may be a call and inward prompting of the Holy Spirit, and I believe that a call is often attended with such an influence which is needed to overcome the strong shrinking which is felt. The only course to take through this extremely delicate and solemn exercise is to *wait* and *pray* and *watch*. If indeed what you felt on the past Lord's Day was a moving of the Holy Spirit you will probably find that though the blessing as such may, in the feeling of it, somewhat subside, it will leave a remaining exercise and leading towards the ministry. This will deepen and clarify, and you may have confirmation of it in other ways, and that would much strengthen and settle your mind. On the other hand, you may feel that though it may be the Lord's will for you to go forth, it is not yet.

I feel I ought to say that I have not been without some feeling that there were indications in your case that you would be sent forth, and I don't think I am alone in that.

I feel there is no need for me to refer to the solemn nature of the work of the ministry, or the need of a gracious preparation for it, and call to it, for I am sure that those considerations weigh upon your mind. I can only seek to pray that the Lord's will may be made clear, and that He may give you grace, as also to us all, to follow Him only.

With my love to you and your dear wife,

Your affectionate pastor, S Delves

As a married pastor he knew something of the trials and self-denials of a pastor's wife and wrote very warmly to one of his lady members whose husband had just been called to a Pastorate and who was troubled by a feeling of rebellion at the prospect of being a pastor's wife.

September 1962.

My dear D.,

I am sorry not to have answered your letter or had opportunity of speaking to you about it. I can truly say how much I understand and enter sympathetically into the difficulties of your present path and your feelings with regard to them.

But if the Lord appoints a certain way for us, however much we might desire another, in due time He will give a willing spirit to accept it and also the grace and help we need to walk in it... but if, as I hope and believe, the Lord's blessing will rest on you both in your new sphere we shall all rejoice in that..

You would naturally feel unequal to the position even as D.. does, but not more than my wife and I did. But 'Hitherto hath the Lord helped us', and so you will find it. A pastor's life makes greater demands on himself, his wife, and his home than is generally realised, but with the Lord's blessing on the labour involved in it, it is a great privilege to serve Him and the flock of God in this way.

It is an encouragement to me, to feel the Lord still directs me in preaching, not only to preach the word in general, but to be the messenger in His message, in a personal way, and that the Lord's word to Peter (John 21.22b) was seasonable and effectual in your present case. I thank you for writing to me.

Most heartily I wish you all the Lord's blessing in the present and the future.

Your affectionate pastor,

S. Delves.

☆ ☆ ☆ ☆ ☆

Searching for some detailed account of Mr Delves' view of the ministry led to some notes written very early in his life as a preacher, maybe even before he began to preach, but they vividly portray his exalted and scriptural view of what preaching should be. First is a quotation from the writings of John Berridge.

Study not to be a fine preacher, Jerichos are blown down with ram's horns. Look simply unto Jesus for preaching food, and what is wanted will be given, and what is given will be blessed, whether it be a barley grain or a wheaten loaf, a crust or a crumb. Your mouth will be a fountain sealed or a flowing stream according as your heart is. Avoid all controversy in preaching or writing or talking, preach nothing down but the devil, and nothing up but Jesus Christ.

Then follows a series of unsigned notes which bear a striking resemblance to remarks in a booklet by E.M. Bound, entitled *"Power through Prayer"* but whether his own or copied they surely represent his own desires and ambitions in the ministry.

There is sometimes somewhat in preaching that cannot be ascribed either to matter or expression and cannot be described what it is or from where it cometh, but with a sweet violence it pierceth into the heart and affections and cometh immediately from the Lord. But if there be any way to obtain such a thing it is by the heavenly disposition of the speaker.

We call it unction. Often earnestness is mistaken for this unction. He who has the Divine Unction will be earnest in the very spiritual nature of things, but there may be a vast deal of earnestness without the least mixture of unction.

What of unction? It is the indefinable in preaching which makes it *preaching*.

It makes the preaching sharp to those who need sharpness, it distils as the dew to those who need to be refreshed.

This unction comes to the preacher not in the study but in the closet. It is Heaven's distillation in answer to prayer.

How and whence comes this unction? Direct from God in answer to prayer. Praying hearts are the only hearts filled with this holy oil; praying lips only are anointed with the divine unction.

Prayer, much prayer is the price of preaching unction. Prayer, much prayer is the one sole condition of keeping this unction.

Without unceasing prayer the unction never comes to the preacher. Without perseverance in prayer the unction, like the manna kept overnight, breeds worms. How can a man preach who does not get his message fresh from God in the closet?

Alas for the pulpit lips that are untouched by this closet frame.

Talking to men for God is a great thing, but talking to God for man is greater still. Praying makes a preacher a heart preacher. Prayer puts the preacher's heart into his sermon, Prayer puts the preacher's sermon into his heart. A prepared heart is better than a prepared sermon. A prepared heart will make a prepared sermon.

It is impossible to give a detailed account of the pastor's view of what the ministry should be, since he never had cause to write out such an account.* However, those who were privileged to hear his ministry are all agreed that certain fundamental features were always present. He had a consistently serious approach to the work of preaching; for him a flippant and jocular approach was anathema, and yet his ministry was never sombre, his heart was too warm with

*Perhaps the nearest approach to such an account of what the minister should be is found in the sermon on page 150—"The Preaching of the Cross".

the truth of the gospel for his delivery to be artificial. He was a man who lived in the word of God and was wholly governed by its teaching. This led to a warm expository style of ministry in which there was a large measure of spiritual application and gracious encouragement. He once said, "A minister's experience should be behind his preaching to give it authority, not in front of his ministry to call attention to himself', and this principle was most apparent in his own preaching. It was an experiential and experimental ministry in the fullest and most Biblical sense, in which he studiously avoided the ludicrous and misleading spiritualisations of Scripture which some men parade as a kind of special spiritual understanding of Scripture. Mercifully Mr. Delves was delivered from such a special and purely subjective interpretation of the word, believing that "no scripture is of any private interpretation" and that Scripture must be interpreted in the light of the whole pattern of Biblical doctrine.

Yet, he was willing to give a spiritual interpretation to a passage of Old Testament scripture where there was warrant to do so. For instance, when taking the journeying of the children of Israel, he would use such events as were specifically referred to and interpreted in the New Testament. "If I follow that rule", he would say, "I know I am safe". The 119th Psalm was one of his favourite parts of the Bible, in which there are many exhortations to take heed to the Scriptures as God's Word or God's Law and this he did constantly in his preaching. So his ministry was always instructive as he was continually striving to lead his people into a deeper appreciation of the great truths of Scripture.

Since the biblical word 'doctrine' means teaching, it is true to say that his ministry was doctrinal. Undergirding every sermon was the great foundation of biblical truth, and often showing through were the doctrines commonly called the doctrines of grace. For him the great truths of absolute divine sovereignty, unconditional electing love, particular and personal redemption, effectual calling by the power of the Holy Spirit and the final certainty of the salvation of Christ's church were no arid or theological scheme but a cause of constant wonder and delight, a constant strength and encouragement to his own soul, and a constant theme running as a golden thread through his preaching. The crowning delight of his own soul was to preach Christ and it was here that the holy, spiritual anointing he had received was most evident. Eternity alone will reveal how many of his hearers came to love and admire their Saviour more through his preaching.

He avoided the barren wastes of mere theological dispute, but was not afraid to deal with issues which were relevant even if disputed and on one occasion commented:

Reasoning is not preaching. At least, a ministry that is full of reasoning and arguing and argument I do not think really has very much effect. Souls are won to Jesus Christ through the effect of the gospel on their hearts. I feel that preaching is not *offering*. I think it is *proclaiming*, it is *setting forth*, it is *publishing*.

'How beautiful upon the mountains are the feet of him that bringeth good tidings, that publisheth peace; that bringeth good tidings of good, that publisheth salvation; that saith unto Zion, Thy God reigneth!' (Is. 52.7), and preaching is just that.

On the vexed question of prophetic interpretation Mr Delves had little to say, but being very fond of the Isle of Wight he spent a number of holidays there when he often used to sit looking over the waters of the Solent. He said on one occasion that on the other side, various places could be seen clearly in the distance, but he could not tell which were nearer than the others. So with regard to prophecies of the future, he could discern events which would certainly take place, such as the Second Coming of Jesus Christ, the last Judgment and the conversion of the Jews. He could not, however, see exactly the order in which these would occur. In the meantime, however, there still constantly flowed between, the pure waters of the gospel.

For the Pastor at Forest Fold, every service was a time of public worship and he was ever anxious that every part of the service should be conducive to a spirit of worship. Excessive excitement and mere fleshly emotion was banished by his emphasis on the deep spirituality of true worship and on the supreme power and authority of Jesus as the eternal and glorious Son of God. Yet there was no quenching of the spirit of praise and for many in the chapel there was the experience of those amazing joys which come to sinners through a loving union with the eternal God.

His emphasis was consistently upon the need for a real heartfelt religion which was clearly the work of the Holy Spirit. Whilst he shunned the excesses of the charismatic movement he strongly insisted on a personal experience of the power of the Holy Spirit. In a sermon on I Cor. 12.27,* he clearly taught that the extraordinary gifts were given

to confirm the dispensation of the Gospel as to its real divine nature and character,

*See Gospel Tidings Vol. 8.p.1.,

and went on to say:

I feel that, just as the solemn accompaniments of the giving of the law were not continued, so these Pentecostal gifts were not continued.

He also lamented the fact that

there was some disorder in regard to the exercise of these gifts, (at Corinth); it did not conduce to a solemn, reverential, gracious worship of God!

However, he was himself a man greatly gifted by God for the work to which he was called, a man who could discern gifts which God had given to others and a man who was glad to encourage those gifted men and women in his congregation to be occupied in those works for which God had fitted them.

It is not without significance that the one or two who insisted very much on the miraculous and extraordinary gifts of the Spirit being the expected and continuing experience of believers, eventually forsook the Pastor of Forest Fold and went amongst those who called his a dead ministry; and that those who sought the spiritual blessings of repentance, faith, love to Christ and to God, zeal for the truth, and good works as an evidence of spiritual life, clung to this man's ministry and found food for their souls!

He several times told his congregation of a certain man who said, "Well, my religion died when Mr. -- died", and warned them against such a religion. He exhorted them never to forget that the minister was only the instrument that the Lord used, saying, "I want Stanley Delves to disappear when I preach and for Jesus only to be exalted".

He knew the trials and perplexities of the ministry and towards the end of his pastorate he wrote to friends mentioning his sense of deep need in preaching.

1. December. 1976.

Dear J. & M.,

Your kind birthday gift to me is most useful and acceptable. I was getting short of handkerchiefs so it was just what I needed and they are such nice ones. It was kind and thoughtful of you and I am very grateful.

Also for the card and the gracious feelings expressed in it.

I felt rather confused on Sunday and quite done up after the services, but I had a quiet restful day on Monday and felt much better, and much enjoyed the gifts and cards which loving friends had given. In a sense Monday was the birthday as my mind was free to think over the memories of the past.

Little did I think when I first entered Forest Fold that my future life and ministry would be centred there, or that such a long pastorate was

99

appointed for me. We have had trials and sorrows during the years we have been together, but what evidences we have had of the Lord's favour resting on us in making His work to appear and establishing the work of our hands upon us thus far.

I have been greatly favoured in the prayerful and loyal affection you and others have felt to me. What a comfort and support this has been words cannot express.

I am one of the most helpless of ministers in myself and have felt to have come to the end of all my ability, even to think anything, times without number, but help has been given just sufficient for the day.

My time cannot be long now and others of our age no doubt feel the same. What a blessing if we are favoured to finish our course with joy.

I am sure you feel as I do, so glad to see J. come along on Sunday evenings. It does stimulate a prayer that he may experience a new birth through hearing the word. What a breakthrough it would be.

Perhaps it is best not to say much at present but to watch and pray.

With much love to you both

S. Delves.

Visiting a chapel in the Midlands (Ebenezer, Old Hill) he was entertained by the pastor, Mr. Harold Crowter. Prior to the evening service at which he was to preach he withdrew as usual for private meditation. It was the custom for him to select a closing hymn in keeping with his subject, but the time passed until the pastor knocked on his door and quietly entering asked whether he was ready. "O Harold", he said, "I'm all confused, it can hardly be time yet". Yet despite such perplexity, he could then proceed to preach a most orderly and gracious sermon lasting almost an hour.

Speaking at another Midlands chapel (Zion, Leicester) he read, prayed and then listened attentively as the deacon announced the second hymn, the subject of which was the true Vine. He commenced his sermon by saying he had had two subjects on his mind, and the hymn just given out had confirmed which subject he was to take. He discoursed freely for over three-quarters of an hour on union to Jesus Christ, and concluded thus, with a satisfied smile on his face saying, "And I think I have taken the right subject!"

In his ministry he avoided sweeping generalisations which could not be substantiated but on occasions would make some general analysis of the condition of religious life in England as he viewed it and in a sermon from Luke 4.18* he comments on evangelical religion at that time.

*Tape published by the Stanley Delves Trust. Second Series, No.3. The sermon was originally preached on 14 July 1978.

It is, I feel, good to be broken-hearted because it tends to a deeper state of heart and mind with regard to our religion. My friends, I think one feature, one very unfavourable feature, of the generality of evangelical religion today, is that it lacks depth. There is a lack of depth. The heart is not sufficiently affected. It tends too much to be the adoption of an evangelical faith rather than a deep and personal experience of the life and power and grace of the gospel in the soul. Superficiality in religion is not good — it may be sincere as far as it goes — I believe it often is as far as it goes, but it is too much on the surface; there is not very much real depth of experience or faith or love in that. We can only really know Jesus Christ, brethren, as He deals graciously with our hearts — we can only know a remedy as it heals us — we can only know power as it acts in our souls and we can only know the preciousness of Jesus Christ as He really heals conditions in our hearts.

Again in a letter to friends in 1968 he comments on the sad lack of evidence of a really godly revival.

January 1968

My beloved friends,

I am sorry that I have been so long in my reply to your very kind letter. I think that I must be slowing down for I always seem to be behind with things these days.

I did so much appreciate your letter and I thank you very much indeed for the photos. I am especially pleased with the one taken at the Chapel doors as it keeps in my eye the friends I have come to love so well over the years. I am sorry, Mr. H.. that you are not on it. I find it hard to give up my visits to my friends in different parts, but I feel the time has come for me to draw in. I am doing it gradually one at a time.

Almost all of my early contempories in the ministry have passed away, and I have reached the evening of life. My chief concern now is to live near the Lord and to finish my course with joy, and the ministry, the gospel which I believe I have received of the Lord Jesus, to testify the gospel of the grace of God.

I hope that this new year may be a time of favour to Zion and to you as a people at B....

The outlook in many ways is dark and depressing. But the Lord reigneth and nothing can prevent the fulfilling of the purposes of His grace.

It has often been the case that a dark time has preceded a time of spiritual awakening and revival. The tide ebbs before the flow. Godliness has been on the ebb in our homeland all of this century and although there are some encouraging signs, I see nothing amounting to a godly revival.

We are well maintained as a people at Forest Fold though just now there is quite a wave of illness and in some cases serious.

I send my love please to R. and B. also Mr and Mrs M. and the friends. The grace of the Lord Jesus Christ be with your spirit,

Yours very affectionately.

S. Delves.

☆ ☆ ☆ ☆ ☆ ☆

In Particular Baptist Churches deacons play an important role which is both practical and spiritual, and unhappily in some instances the Biblical distinction between the office of deacon and the office of elder is sadly obscured as deacons become unappointed and sometimes unwanted ruling elders. Such a confusion did not arise at Forest Fold and a loving and loyal relationship existed between the Pastor and deacons. During the long pastorate eleven new deacons were appointed at various times to replace those who had been taken home and at the end five still held office, five who have had to carry the full burdens of responsibility alone now for three years. (March 1981)

Letters written at various times through the pastorate indicate his loving concern for his deacons and the encouragement he gave them.

20 September 1948.

My dear Friend and Brother,

The voting of the members in the matter of appointing more deacons has resulted in the choice of you and Mr... to fill that office amongst us. Fifty-four votes were given for your name and forty-five for Mr... The result is as I felt it would be and now I am free to say that your appointment is most acceptable to me and I believe the other deacons. At the same time I have desired to be impartial in my remarks before the members, and I hope none will feel that there is any dis-esteem for them. I desire to feel the same regard and affection for each of our members.

As holding office in the Church of God, it is laid upon us to seek to devote ourselves to its interests in the faith and order of the Gospel, by steadfastness, wisdom, and affection, to promote unity and peace among the members and the furtherance of the gospel as the Lord may enable. I know that this has been your desire and prayer during the years that you and Mrs... have been members of the Church, and you have been helped to manifest that spirit which has caused us to feel that we can safely ask you to undertake this further responsibility. And may it be the Lord's will to continue both you and Mrs... to the Church for years to come in usefulness and happiness.

If there is time next Saturday evening I will bring the matter forward, and it is usual after I have said a few words for one of the Deacons to add a few words and then for the member appointed to reply. But I think it doubtful if there will be time; if not the matter will fall on the quarterly meeting on Monday October 4.

I will not add more to this note which is only intended to inform you of the results.

I send my deep tender affection to you in the Lord's name.

Yours very sincerely,

S. Delves.

The building that was Durrants, the grocer's in the Pantiles where
Stanley Delves worked: the top right window was his lodging where
he felt his call to Forest Fold confirmed by the Lord.

Little Dicker Chapel, where Stanley Delves preached his first sermon

Chapel House, Forest Fold, with hall and bathroom added during
Mrs. Delves' latter years.

Forest Fold.

Undated.

My dear. Mr...

A few remarks you made to me in the vestry the other Sunday prompt me to send this short letter, especially because I believe you have said something the same before. I think that you distress your mind unduly because you feel that you have not the ability of utterance in public prayer and in other ways, that some have. As you stand in the position of a senior deacon you probably feel that all the more. I am sorry if you do. It is not given to all to have the same readiness to speak and to take the lead in difficult matters that arise in churches. Neither is it necessary. You have been given grace to fill your position as a member for many years, and as a deacon, in other and more useful ways. I will only mention for one thing how much you have done in a practical way for both the Chapels but especially at Forest Fold.

But more particularly you have truly been a pillar in the church by your steadfast, loyal and humble spirit. I have always felt and more increasingly as the years have gone on that I could rely on you and Mrs... as comfortably as anyone among us. I could wish for nothing more than that all of our members should be as stable and unmoveable in their profession and membership with all the duties and responsibilities connected with it as by the grace of God you have been. You have been a strength to our cause and a great help and comfort to me.

Also I always feel that you show much wisdom in your choice of hymns. They are a most important part of our worship. Suitable and savoury hymns add much to the service and to the feelings of the friends in singing them. They have to sing the hymns that are chosen for them, and if they are not expressive of their feelings it doesn't go so well. It isn't every hymn in our book that is suitable for all to sing. I believe that the choice of hymns is a prayerful concern to you which accounts for the way your mind is led, and the blessing that rests on the hymns you choose.

In these and in other ways you fill your position among us most usefully and acceptably, and I do hope you may be spared to the cause for years to come. Also your prayers are as acceptable to God as any which are offered among us, for He knows how our hearts feel and regards that more than the ability with which we can express ourselves. It's not gift but grace that prevails in prayer.

I hope you will believe me to be sincere when I say that you have been a blessing to Forest Fold, and there is no reason for you to feel any insufficiency other than we all feel who occupy any position in the church of God and I most of all. The time is fast hastening on when our work will be done. I hope that others will be raised up to take our place and Forest Fold may be a favoured place in the future as it has been in the past.

There is no need to reply to this,

With my love and esteem,

S. Delves.

Church life at Forest Fold was directed by a pastor whose great concern was to follow the word of God in all its gracious precepts, and to follow it in the spirit of love and harmony. He had a healthy fear of sterile debates about the "commandments and doctrines of men", being convinced that there was sufficient teaching in the Scriptures for the formation and guidance of Gospel churches. He was not a strong advocate of denominational rules and regulations. This does not mean that he was in any way 'loose' in his leadership as pastor of the church, but he considered it better to be guided by the Scriptures themselves than by rules made by men. His reasons for this were that during his ministry he had made many contacts with other pastors and deacons, and had been called upon to give advice on so many occasions. Through these experiences he learned enough to realise that difficulties often arose because of a blind adherence to rules and regulations, or dogmatic interpretations of such rules. He saw that divisions could so often have been avoided if the spirit of gospel fellowship had prevailed amongst members of the spiritual body of Jesus Christ. He often stressed the need of forbearance between church members as being "members in particular" of that mystical body of Christ and the need to remember that all church members are still imperfect sinners saved by grace.

One aspect of church life and pastoral responsibility which caused Mr Delves a life-long anxiety was the conducting of church meetings. One of his daughters commented on his concern in this connection:

If Father took his pastoral responsibilities very seriously, and we know he did, then the ministry was a continual burden. He often used to say that he always seemed to be living with a sermon looming up in front of him and as soon as that was gone there was another. Visiting was a strain and he laboured at this with an unjustifiable feeling of inadequacy, but the hardest part of being a pastor to him was, I think, church meetings.

With regard to meetings to hear testimonies, amidst his feelings of joy and thankfulness, his care for his flock sometimes made even these occasions a strain. But the routine meetings he always approached with fear and dread. At the end of his 54-year pastorate one Sunday evening he sat back in his chair with the greatest imaginable relief and said, "Now I shall not have to go to any more Church Meetings". I think this great fear of these meetings sprang from two things. Soon after the commencement of his public profession, he lived through the experience of a church dividing and eventually separating. One can imagine that to a young man with a tender spirit, deeply taught and constantly meditating in the things of the gospel, perhaps even at that age having an insight into the gospel principles of church love and fellowship, to find turmoil and fighting and enmity where he had expected to find love and respect and a walking in the fear of the Lord, probably left him scarred in that particular area of Christian experience. The sadness and the dread of ever experiencing another such situation never left him.

Secondly, because of his extensive ministry and the great affection in which he was held in the churches where he visited and the homes where he was entertained, he was also the confidant of many friends regarding church matters — more than anyone could ever imagine, I rather suspect. He therefore knew more than most of the unhealthy, as well as the prosperous nature of life in many of the churches, and throughout his long association with these churches had known very much of the troubles which had come upon them. He felt very keenly the dishonour it was to the name of Jesus Christ and the sadness and sorrow which came upon many of those who loved and followed Him, when they were so divided among themselves.

This fear of similar evils coming into his own beloved church and among his flock was never far from his mind, and this accentuated his dread of church meetings. His experience and observation had shown him that trouble could arise from comparatively insignificant matters, and with differing personalities and priorities, could easily escalate if not handled with wisdom and in the fear of the Lord.

This excessive fear of church meetings was not so apparent to his church members as to his family, and many have testified to the benefit and blessings received from his remarks at such meetings. One of the members comments:

On the first church meeting of the new year, our pastor would give us a short address which embodied so much, and I felt was conducted with great wisdom. The blessings of the past year were related concerning the Church. We were given guidance and counsel, exhortations and advice on how members should act. This was all given in such a manner that our hearts were warmed with love for our pastor and the church.

Another member writes;

He was given grace to handle matters wisely, his very spirit through grace hating controversy or lengthy discussions, and he would refrain from entering in on any matter likely to offend or hurt, yet he always dealt faithfully. The honour of God and the good of souls was all he sought.

There were meetings of a painful nature. These affected him much, before, at the time, and afterwards; but most were peaceful and blessed occasions.

Much warmth of love and kindred spirit flowed in our Church meetings; pastor often expressed appreciations, often counselled us, warned us, and encouraged us.

He would often turn business meetings to prayers; these were favoured times.

A few interesting extracts from the church minute book give some indication of the ability which the Pastor was given to guide and counsel his church through many problems:

3. October 1969

It was mentioned that the previous Lord's day was the fiftieth anniversary of the baptism of ten members at Forest Fold, who were shortly followed by three others. Of these, seven remain faithful members but some had passed away.

2. April 1962

Pastor spoke of the solemn responsibilities of Church membership both toward God, toward the Church and toward them that are without, and the need of great wisdom, prudence and the fear of God in all our ways.

After receiving in two members he said this applied to us each, We do well to ask ourselves how we were walking, what guides us, Christ's law or a law to ourselves? Have we a hard spirit, a beam in our eye, or are we walking to the Lord's honour and glory? We need kind and tender watchfulness.

2. February 1965

Attention was drawn to two longstanding members, one for 56 years and one for 51 years, and of their faithful and gracious loyalty to the cause and consistent walk and conversation.

2. January 1967

The Pastor read a letter received from a local minister relating to a united meeting on Church unity involving all sects. He read a reply to the effect that while we esteem spiritual union and fellowship where it can be enjoyed, we could not in any way associate ourselves with this movement.

10. July 1967

The Pastor mentioned the unrest and divisions appearing in some Churches and his concern that the peace and unity we enjoy might be preserved among us.

15. July 1974

Pastor mentioned that on the past Lord's Day there was a general feeling that the Lord's blessing was with us and he felt we have cause for thanksgiving, but we needed to walk humbly. Felt we were favoured with prosperity. Prayer needed for showers of blessing and that the Lord might direct the hearts of others to join. Not to grieve or quench the Holy Spirit. Felt both thankfulness and concern.

10. March 1977

Pastor spoke thankfully of peace and unity in the Church through all the years.

9

A Brother Beloved

The Pastor, the father, the man, and his interests

"All my state shall Tychicus declare unto you, who is a beloved brother, and a faithful minister and fellow servant in the Lord"

Col. 4.7.

Those who gathered at Forest Fold had a true pastor, a man of compassion and a man of prayer. One of those who valued this blessing has written the following brief testimony:

When Mr. Delves was visiting in the area where I live, he would sometimes come to our home for lunch, a nap and a little chat. Never any gossip or unkind words about people, but his talk so often centred on Jesus Christ. Of course, he had failings and little odd ways (haven't we all!) but he lived as near his Lord as any man I have ever known. He so often made me long to be holy.

Our loved Pastor was one of the very few people I could spiritually confide in and he always understood, even me. He oft refreshed my spirit, and would encourage the very weakest.

I was very touched one day when talking about prayer, he suddenly said; "I have written down the names of my entire congregation grouping them in families. In the order in which they come on my list, I especially desire to remember them at different times during the day, praying for them each personally". He added, "I felt I was always praying for the Church as a whole or for special cases, but felt perhaps I was neglecting some. Now today, I have Mr. and Mrs. C. on my heart and have really found it very sweet committing them to the Lord, and thanking Him for them: for Mrs. C's gracious, loving membership amongst us and for Mr. C's loyal, quiet walk, neither ever causing the slightest trouble in our midst."

He said that he was very inclined to muddle two of the young men in one family, but that when he had written down their names he could see them very clearly in his mind.

A few minutes after he had told me this, he said, "Oh, I have never mentioned this to anybody before — it sounds just as if I'm saying, 'What a good boy am I'. But the Lord alone knows how I feel."

Another time whilst talking about prayer, he said that often he would wake up about 2 o'clock in the morning and pray and yearn for the young people. At this time, some were causing him much concern and he said: "Sometimes I feel I shall be taken before I see the answers to many of my prayers: still, the Lord has been wonderfully good."

He was so contented with his little home, and one day he asked if I would like to hear a description of the home he would like when he retired. With a twinkle in his eye, he described in detail his home at Forest Fold and said, "I do hope that I can live and die amongst my own family and people". This request was wonderfully granted.

☆ ☆ ☆ ☆ ☆

One of the tasks which the Lord has committed to real Pastors is that of visiting; indeed, the Lord severely castigates the false pastors who, "have scattered my flock, and driven them away, and have not visited them" (Jeremiah 23.2). To this task the Pastor at Forest Fold set himself despite a deep and unrelieved persuasion that he was quite unsuited for that particular aspect of the ministry. His daughter, Christine, describes something of the personal trial which this work seemed to be.

Visiting, for some reason, seemed to be hard work in the main to my father which was a pity, because his visits were appreciated and, as far as I am aware, usually beneficial and rewarding. It may have been partly because Father saw himself as first, foremost and altogether a minister of the gospel. Most of his time, therefore, was taken with meditation and sermon preparation and that did not leave a great deal of time for visiting and possibly at the time of visiting he was already oppressed with the prospect of the next sermon and anxious to put his mind to its preparation.

Looking back on our early family life, I can remember Monday as being usually a day of unrelieved gloom. I can see now that Father was obviously physically exhausted by the effort of preaching three times the previous day and emotionally drained by the strain involved. It was also usually visiting day which added further darkness to Father's spirit; partly because he did not accomplish as much as he felt he should, partly because he did not feel he did it as well as he should, and partly because he came back like a sponge, having absorbed all the troubles and sorrows and criticisms. The last were particularly tortuous to his spirit — he could not think why so many illnesses were caused by chapel temperatures, too hot, too cold, too draughty, not enough ventilation; why the speed of the singing or other real or imagined mismanagements were so much more important than the content of the sermon, and the faith he so longed to see mixing with it in his hearer's hearts. I can also remember (even as quite a young child) that the one redeeming feature of Monday was the Prayer Meeting. After this meeting, the tension seemed lifted and the gloom gone. There had often been signs of appreciation of the ministry, faith and love in exercise and apparently not *all* the congregation had been stricken down by the invidious illnesses resulting from the Sunday attendance at services!

Father was usually away on Tuesdays and Wednesdays, busy on Thursdays with correspondence and preparation for the evening service so Friday was the next "visiting day". Friday visiting, as I remember it, was not such a wearing exercise. I presume Father by then had recovered from the previous Sunday's strain and was far enough from the coming one to cope. Also he had usually been cheered and stimulated by the affection and kindness of friends where he had ministered, and the break from any troubles at home (which invariably weighed him down) had obviously done him good.

Not all visiting programmes were like this one instance which I quote. But this all actually happened one week in 1974 a few weeks prior to the Jubilee Services, Father being then 76 years old. I was taking him around, and on the Monday morning, to please me, he went first to visit an elderly, but eccentric friend of mine. Although a lover of Jesus Christ she was a very ardent Arminian in outlook. However, Father was pleased to come and see her and to talk to her about Mr. Poole-Connor who had been her Pastor, and under whose pastorate her father had been a deacon. Father had heard Mr. Poole-Connor preach in Tunbridge Wells when about 20 years old and could still remember the sermon and as he had recently been reading a biography of the gentleman, he and my friend had much to discuss. Father, with his usual wisdom and tact brought the visit to a close when he saw the conversation getting to points on which he could see they would differ. We then went to visit another friend who had links with and interests in the Free Evangelical Churches. With her, Father talked with ability of various specific churches and also on the state of the Church of England, the new Archbishop and the various outlooks of many past Archbishops. After a short reading and prayer we left. In the evening we visited a young couple who had recently come to attend at Forest Fold. To them Father spoke very tenderly of their various family concerns, of his pleasure at seeing them at Forest Fold, of his own confidence in the truth of what he believed and preached, and of his concern that it should be experienced in the life and hearts of those to whom he preached and for whom he prayed. This visit terminated with short, but very sweet, reading and prayer.

The next day was Tuesday. The morning Father spent in sermon preparation, and in the afternoon I took him to friends for tea before the evening service. To them he spoke with knowledge and sympathy of various family difficulties and they chatted about the churches in the Midlands. A guest from Scotland was also at the meal-table and, with her, Father discussed St. Giles Cathedral; architecturally, historically and doctrinally with memories of his own visits there.

The third day was Wednesday. Again another evening preaching engagement preceded by tea with other friends. Here Father, able to remember other members of their family by name, could enter into the various details of their lives which included discussion of chapels in the west country; this time geographically (with incredible detail), and denominationally, and many of the people attending them.

It seemed to me that after these differing and widely varying types of visiting, it should be easy to convince Father that his felt inadequacy in visiting was but a myth. But I do not think he ever felt competent in that field.

☆ ☆ ☆ ☆ ☆

At Forest Fold it had been a long tradition for parents blessed with the gift of children to bring their babies, as soon as possible, to the chapel to give thanks to God for precious life given and for the returning health of the mother. On such occasions their Pastor would come from the pulpit to take the baby in his arms, tell the congregation the name chosen by the parents and then pray most feelingly for God's blessing on the child. When naming a baby, he would always be very careful to make sure that no one in his congregation thought that there was any merit in it, but he would pray very earnestly for the parents, that they might be able to bring the child up in the admonition of the Lord, and that God would grant the child grace in later years to believe in the Lord Jesus Christ as their own Redeemer. How many of these prayers were wonderfully answered long afterwards, the church books at Forest Fold, and in many other places would reveal. Many named at Forest Fold are named in the Lamb's book of life, to the praise of Jesus' name.

☆ ☆ ☆ ☆ ☆

Children responded warmly to his love and especially because he could so readily enter into their interests and pleasures. One time his grandson was supposedly fishing out of a window of the new Sunday school building, and grandad was seen to crawl along and fix an apple to the lad's line! Such was his nature, warm, loving, and ever willing to enter into the joys and sorrows of others.

It was during the early part of the war — 1941 — when one of the Forest Fold boys, nine year old Keith Fermor, was walking down the road with his sister and, stepping off the verge, was knocked over by an army lorry and instantly killed. This was a very deep blow to all the Chapel 'family' at Forest Fold, and, of course, particularly to the immediate family. The Pastor was a great comfort to them all at that time, and took for his text the following Sunday (10 August) "Is it well with the child? And she answered, It is well" (II Kings 4:26). The following is the short address given at the funeral so vividly illustrating the Pastor's gracious ability to speak suitably in such circumstances.

It is a sad occasion viewed from our standpoint, that has brought us together this afternoon. Mercifully, and by the good providence of God, it is rare that our children are taken from us, but in this case God has permitted it to be so. Secondary causes shall not now be spoken of. "It is the LORD: let him do what seemeth him good". That was spoken by one of old whose heart was grieved and broken, and it is good to feel able to say that. It is not a fatalistic thing to say, for where 'it is the LORD' there is wisdom, there is love, there is compassion, and there is also a purpose. O, that we may have grace to bow to that and to say 'The LORD gave, the LORD hath taken away; blessed be the name of the LORD'.

There is no need for me to speak at this moment of the love, the sympathy and the sorrow that we feel for our friends. They have had abundant evidence of that. I never felt in myself, and I have never seen, such a manifestation of the truth of that Scripture that, speaking of the union of heart and spirit that there is between those that are one in the Lord, says

"And whether one member suffer, all the other members suffer with it". I believe there is a love between us here as members one of another that makes our feelings exceed that natural sympathy that is felt by all who have any humanity in them, on such occasions. It is that love and union that makes our brother's and sister's grief to be our own; it makes us feel that we have lost one because they have.

We loved little Keith. He had so many ways that endeared him to us that, at this moment, I cannot trust myself to speak much. It must be sufficient to say this, that we have a real persuasion that the Lord prepared the little lad for the close of his short life. Many of the ways of God, as far as he understood them, were very evident. And now the Lord has been pleased to bring this life to a close when he in his life was but on the very threshold of it. To us, of course it is sad; yet there are several things that we might fasten on to relieve our sadness. He is taken, we know not from what; he is taken, we cannot fully understand what to. The Lord has been pleased to take him into His harbour, secure from the winds and storms of temptation that cause so many to make shipwreck of their immortal souls.

Well, we would feel thankful that he never grew up if it should have been so — which, of course, we cannot say; thankful that he never grew up to give himself up to the ways of death as so many do. And Jesus called a little child unto Him and said, "For of such is the Kingdom of God." And we believe it of him. The Lord has been gracious to our friends. They have proved that there is in the grace and love of Jesus Christ that which sweetens and sustains, which produces reconciliation to His will and which strengthens faith and love to bear these things. It has not been sorrow with no mixture of sweetness in it.

These things have a voice, only we are so slow to hear that which is spoken. If we could hear the voice of the silent form, it might be somewhat as Another, even the Son of God, "Weep not for me, but weep for yourselves." He might speak to such as might grow up to live without God and without hope in the world, to perish at the last; and he might say, "It is your case that is sad, not mine".

The pastor loved the children of his congregaton and lived to see some of the babies he had named grow up, to marry them, to baptize them and to see them joining in the fellowship of the church, to name their babies and so on into the next generation. In fact there are two families at Forest Fold who have seen four generations in the church, all of whom had been baptized by their Pastor.

There is an active Sunday School at Forest Fold which has been superintended by a succession of able and gracious men. This work the Pastor constantly encouraged and would often give a children's address. When his strength was failing he could no longer do what he formerly did in the Sunday School, but retained a most warm interest in its work, writing the following letter to a friend about to become a teacher in the school:

My dear D...,

I intended before this to write this note about you taking a class in our Sunday School but with my backwardness in writing it has been delayed. I am thankful that you feel able with the Lord's help to undertake this service amongst the children.

It is a privilege and a responsibility to undertake any duty in His cause whatever way and sphere may be appointed to us. And if we may be the means in His hand of speaking a word which to young or old may be made a blessing, it is all we desire. It is not an easy matter to speak to children, yet the mind is often more impressionable during that formative period of life and a word received at that time often comes into life in after years, and is probably never entirely obliterated.

I am sorry I am not able to give more time to the children, but the constant exercise and labour of the ministry takes all of my mind and strength, and I feel that is my calling. So I am very thankful we have other friends among us who have the grace and affection for them and our cause at Forest Fold, and willingness of mind to undertake that work.

May the Lord bless each one in it and make their labour of love most useful among the rising generation, whom we hope and pray will take the place of us older ones in future years.

I thank you D... very much for your promise. May the Lord bless your instruction and give you every encouragement in it. And may we all be enabled by the grace of God to cleave together in love one to another, and to the Truth as it is in Jesus abounding therein with thanksgiving.

With my love to D... and my best wishes to you all.

S. Delves.

Handicrafts were started about 1948 in a member's home, and the Pastor was always interested in the items which were made for the local Sale of Work for the Aged Pilgrims' Friend Society. In later years it was held each Friday evening in the Sunday School, and the custom was at the close to have a short story for the children and a hymn and prayer. Whenever he was indoors and available he would come across to the brief ending – cast a loving and admiring glance over any work the children showed him and close the meeting with prayer. This, the children loved. Sometimes he would tell them about his time in the Army during the first world war, and although he felt he could not speak to children, they all enjoyed his talks. One Friday he was asked for a story, but felt unable, so it was put off until the following week. He must have been very sorely tried about this story and prayed much regarding it. When the time came, he spoke about Jeremiah being cast into the pit, and how he was pulled out, and the children had to guess where the story came from and the man's name. This was made a great blessing to one of the young helpers and she was enabled to realise that she had been pulled out of the pit and had been made free by the cleansing blood of Christ — what an answer to his many prayers during the week.

He liked to remember children's names, especially those in the families where he stayed. He would write them all in his pocket book and then say with glee, "They will be so surprised next year when I remember all their names".

Once, just before Christmas, he overheard a little girl say to her mother as he passed them, "Mummy, is that a *real* Father Christmas?". This incident greatly amused him, his eyes twinkled and his shoulders shook with laughter as he recounted it.

☆ ☆ ☆ ☆ ☆

Mr. Delves had the God-given ability to speak suitably and acceptably at any occasion which arose. Wedding ceremonies were no exception, and his affectionate addresses were much appreciated. On one occasion, he departed from his usual course of giving counsel to the bridal couple and gave a memorable address on the following lines based on the marriage of Cana of Galilee:

(1) *Whatever is human may fail.* Human love, like wine, may in time diminish (Mr. Delves added at once that he had no reason to suppose this would happen in the present case).

(2) *When human supplies fail, Jesus can always make up the lack.* If our love declines, Jesus is able to revive it.

(3) *What Jesus gives is always the best.* His love is the very best love.

The following notes of another wedding address were found in his own handwriting and give a vivid picture of his loving concern for those beginning their married life:

There is a very happy aspect to this service this morning and there is also a very solemn aspect to it. You have made solemn declarations and promises as in the sight of God, and may He give you both grace and faithfulness to fulfil them, both in the letter and the spirit.

I am taking three words from what you have repeated together and offering a few comments upon them.

Love, that faculty of our nature whereby we feel to delight in whatever is pleasing and attractive to us. It is good to love and to be loved, and in married life it is essential to all comfort and happiness. This unites you in heart and spirit as well as in body. If you truly love each other you will find more pleasure in each other than in anyone else in the world, and more so as the years go by. True love makes you *unselfish* - turns mutual duties into *mutual pleasures,* and *obligations* into *opportunities.* When love prevails the consideration is not what one can get out of married life, but what one can put into it. Love will make you *forbearing, understanding.*

Honour is the esteem and respect due to what is *good* and *worthy* of respect and of high repute.

(1) *You must be worthy of this honour* - and that applies equally on both sides. There is no need that you should attain to high positions in life, honour is not particularly attached to high estate so much as to high character and principles.

(2) *You must readily give this honour to each other*, and always regard each other with very high esteem. In the home the husband is head, and not only in the home. Never speak of each other but with respect and esteem.

Cherish is to *help, support* and *comfort* with tenderness and affection.

(1) *There will be much occasion for you to cherish one another, sorrows, illness*, possibly *trials* in life of one kind and another, besides your affections need to be cherished.

(2) *There are many ways in which you may cherish* -

(i) By *your tender thoughtful spirit*

(ii) By *word* and *deed*

Now I have put before you the way of a happy married life. But having done this, I will direct your minds to the best counsel of all, even to the holy Word of God in which you may find profitable instruction and counsel.

It would be right to comment here that Mr. Delves regularly noted down his thoughts regarding such wedding addresses, also, after his death, a large number of notes of sermons were found in his study. These he made in the course of meditation and were evidently the secret of his orderly manner of speaking. However he never used these notes when actually speaking or preaching, they were simply made to fix the order of his subject in his mind.

☆ ☆ ☆ ☆ ☆

To those who were facing life with all its prospects, for the young men and women of the congregation, he had a great concern, a concern portrayed in a short letter to one of his young friends:

December 1935.

My dear M,

I hope that you are getting on comfortably and feel happy in your new work. I was very glad to see you on Sunday and I hope that you will still be able to come regularly as you have done in the past. I am writing this letter to you because I want to say one or two things which I haven't seemed to be able to say to you personally. As I have said before, I very sincerely hope that you will be happy where you are now, and that in all your future life you may be helped and blessed of God. But what I am very concerned to know is whether the Lord has blessed you and will bless you in spiritual things. If it should be so, it will not only be the greatest good that can ever come to you but it will make your life useful in the church of God, and what a day that would be to me and others who pray for you very often. For I can assure you that you and your sister and all the young people are very near my heart. There is no time like our early years to seek the Lord and the saving knowledge of His truth.

None who have done so, through grace, have ever wished they had wasted their early years in sin and worldliness, whilst others who have been brought back from such ways have always felt ashamed when they have remembered their lost years. If that day comes, which I hope and pray that it may, when you will find it in your heart to say "Thy people shall be my people, and thy God my God," it will be an answer to many prayers. It is a great thing to have a love to the ways of God, and also an ear to hear His truth which is able to save our souls. If our beginnings seem to be small yet that is nothing against us, because if it is a right beginning the Lord will gradually deepen His work in our hearts and teach us to know more of Him and of His truth. It is usually little by little that we are taught of God and after many years we feel to know very little. It is a great thing to know God at all and to have it in our hearts to pray and seek after Him.

Your affectionate friend,

S. Delves

The following is an autograph written in 1949 in a young friend's album:

"The Lord is my shepherd, I shall not want"
for
Rest   "He maketh me to lie down in green pastures"
Restoration "He restoreth my soul"
Protection "I will fear no evil for thou art with me"
Provision   "I will dwell in the house of the Lord for ever"
With my loving wishes for all the above to my very dear friend Joyce

Stanley Delves
28 August 1949

☆ ☆ ☆ ☆ ☆

The pastoral care of the flock involved him in the many inevitable sorrows which this fallen world is constantly facing, and it was at times of sickness and bereavement that his people rightly turned to him for sympathy and help. In spite of an almost obsessive feeling of inadequacy for this aspect of pastoral care, Mr. Delves was given a special grace to enter so feelingly into the needs of his families and could indeed "weep with those who weep". His life of many personal illnesses, his wife's weakness and the bereavements he suffered were all part of the Lord's furnace in which the gold was refined, so that the Pastor at Forest Fold could obey that ancient commission, "Comfort ye, comfort ye my people, saith your God".

It is hard to select from so many records of funeral addresses and memorial services but the following extracts from a memorial sermon preached in 1960 on the death of a deacon, Samuel George Hoad, will illustrate what was so typical of his ministry on such occasions, sympathizing, encouraging and teaching. The text was:

"Therefore, my beloved brethren, be ye stedfast, unmoveable, always abounding in the work of the Lord, forasmuch as ye know that your labour is not in vain in the Lord." I Cor. 15.58.

How suitable a word this is as a tribute to our brother because the features of my text appeared unusually clear in his case. He was stedfast, he was unmoveable, and he was *useful.* And not only useful amongst us as a people where his heart always was fixed in its affections, but useful also in the work of the Lord in other places of truth as well.

Also, I feel here is a most suitable word for ourselves.

"Therefore, my beloved brethren, be ye stedfast, unmoveable." This is always suitable, but when pillars are removed from the Church of God, I mean from any particular and individual church, when any who have stood firm and stedfast are taken home, all the more need that those who remain should seek to be more stedfast because of the loss of a pillar from the Church of God. For if one pillar after another is removed and there is not stedfastness in those that remain, what is going to happen? The house will fall! and it is as likely to fall if it is a large house as a small one, for the number of members in a church is no guarantee of its continuation. What is so necessary is stedfastness. Twenty members, in a church, who are stedfast and unmoveable, secure that church by the grace of God more than forty who are unstable.

And so, I feel in our present case this is a most needful word because such a stedfast member has been removed from us. What is more, I can see that this word this morning would be just what our brother would wish me to bring before you, because I know his exercise, and how he felt about matters — his anxiety sometimes — and I know how concerned he was for our stedfastness in the truth.

Let us then, as the Lord may enable, apply our minds to this Word.

Now it is the practical concluson of a very remarkable and wonderful, and most blessed chapter in which the apostle was led to defend and expound the doctrine of the resurrection of the dead..... and a very vital doctrine he makes that to be. The occasion of his writing so fully upon it was because there were some amongst the Corinthian members who denied the resurrection.

"How say some among you that there be no resurrection of the dead?" It is surprising really, how soon the tares of error sprang up where the apostles had sown the good seed of truth. But it was so, and although that in itself was an evil, it worked for good in this sense, that it occasioned that defence of truth in the epistles which has been such a blessing to the Church of God all down the ages since those days. If there had been none amongst the Corinthians who had denied the resurrection, speaking naturally, the apostle would not have been led to have written such a beautiful chapter of truth with regard to it. And what a comfort this Word has been to countless mourners when they have seen their loved ones, at least the bodies of their loved ones, laid in the grave, to feel that it is only till He comes. The doctrine of the resurrection of the body is a blessed light upon the darkness of the tomb.

Now I would have you observe this point, that every part of truth is inseparable: it must stand or fall together. It is more than probable that those at Corinth who said there was no resurrection of the dead, did not realise how far their error extended, "But", said the apostle in substance, "the resurrection of the dead and the resurrection of Jesus Christ are inseparable, and if you deny the one you imply your faith is vain, you are yet in your sins. "Then they also which are fallen asleep in Christ are perished", for errors of any kind usually extend a very great deal farther than those who perpetrate them realise.

And so, the apostle was led first to defend the doctrine of the resurrection upon the foundation of the resurrection of Jesus Christ. He said, "Moreover, brethren, I declare unto you the gospel which I preached unto you and wherein ye stand." And in substance it was this: "That Christ died for our sins according to the Scriptures: that He was buried, and that He rose again the third day according to the Scriptures." There, very simply put, are the fundamentals of the gospel of our faith, our hope of everything we profess. The resurrection of Jesus Christ is the foundation of the resurrection of the Church of God, and so He said Himself "I am the resurrection and the life."

There was great need for the apostle to give such prominence to that, and actually, there is more prominence given to the resurrection in the New Testament than there is to the separate state of the souls of those who die in the Lord. There is no doubt about that however, because the apostle said for himself, and there is no reason whatever to feel that it was exclusive to him alone. "I am willing rather to be absent from the body and to be present with the Lord." That is all we need to know with regard to the state of the souls of the departed in the Lord. They are present with Him: they are freed from all the limitations, weaknesses, frailties and sorrows that pertain to this our present life: they are joined in that blessed, celestial company of the spirits of just men made perfect. But we do not read so much with regard to that, as with regard to the resurrection of the body, and I should feel for this reason, that the resurrection of the body is a truth peculiar to the gospel. Whereas, even in those days, many who did not believe, or indeed, knew nothing about the gospel, believed that the soul existed apart from the body. Of course, they would have no knowledge of the blessed existence as the gospel reveals it. For instance, when the apostle stood on Mars Hill, Athens, and delivered that noble defence of truth, they heard him fairly patiently until he came to the resurrecton and when he spoke of the resurrection of the dead some mocked. Now, if he had spoken of a separate state of the soul they would not have mocked, because that was one of their doctrines. They believed that, but when he spoke of the resurrection of the dead some mocked. That was a doctrine that they had never heard of and did not believe possible. Therefore, because the resurrection of the dead is such an essential gospel truth and doctrine it is given such prominence. The apostle not only defends the doctrine, resting it upon the resurrection of Jesus Christ, but he expounds it. He anticipates an objection. If the objection is made in a sceptical sense, it indicates folly. If the question is asked, "How are the dead raised up? and with what body do they come?", in a sceptical way, the answer is, "Thou fool", or in other words "Thou foolish one". But if the question is asked in a right spirit then the answer is, "Well, in the resurrection there is identity". It is the same body, the body with which they come is their own body, even as the patriarch Job seems to have envisaged it: "And though after my skin worms destroy this body, yet in my flesh shall I see God: Whom I shall see for myself, and mine eyes shall behold, and not another; though my reins be consumed within me." Job 19.26. The bodies of the saints in the resurrection will be their own personal bodies. It will be them; that part of them which fell into corruption and decay in death. "It is sown in corruption; it is raised in incorruption; It is sown in dishonour; it is raised in glory:....it is sown a natural body; it is raised a spiritual body," and it is the same 'it'. It is the same 'it' that is raised that was sown.

But while there is identity there is a remarkable change in its character. The same body but not in the same state and condition, nor in the same constitution. The apostle says there is a natural body and there is a spiritual body. Not that there is a spirit but that there is a spiritual body that is not gross, fleshly, material, as our bodies are now, but spiritual. I doubt if anyone has ever been able to understand exactly what a spiritual body is. The nearest we shall ever know this side of the resurrection of what a spiritual body is, must be derived from such indication as we have of the risen body of the Lord Jesus Christ. His risen body was a spiritual body and to the likeness of that spiritual body will all the bodies of the saints be raised in the great resurrection day. The apostle sums it all up in this: "I show you a mystery" — A mystery means something hidden in the mind and purpose of God but which is now made known in the truth of it, but which still retains an element we cannot understand: something beyond our comprehension. It is revealed but it still remains to a great extent incomprehensible to us.

Well now, all this wonderful, blessed, encouraging truth concerning the resurrection the apostle brings to this conclusion: "Therefore, my beloved brethren, be ye stedfast." Seeing that you have such a prospect as this, and seeing that it is confirmed to you by such an unquestionable proof as the resurrection of Jesus Christ, then 'be ye stedfast'. Now, how good and profitable it is when sublime truths like these are brought down to a practical and personal and profitable conclusion. Otherwise, we seem somewhat lost in their mystery, their sublime, incomprehensible character.

☆ ☆ ☆ ☆ ☆

Beyond the limits of his own congregation Mr. Delves had wide interests, never a man to be bound and blinkered by denominational barriers, whilst shunning a false ecumenism which seeks unity at the expense of truth, he did "seek peace and pursue it". His warm and kindly spirit endeared him to many and drew them together across what might otherwise have been impassable barriers of denominational pride or an understandable fear of compromise. He showed that it was possible to maintain the highest standards of integrity in the truth and yet embrace those who truly knew the Lord as fellow members of the body of Christ. This truly Christian charity was but a reflection of the love of Christ Himself, who once said, "For he that is not against us is on our part". This true charity was not blind to another saying of the Lord "He that is not with me is against me; and he that gathereth not with me scattereth abroad", and throughout his ministry he most surely and consistently contended earnestly for the faith.

Amongst his many interests there were a number of interdenominational societies which had his unswerving support. The Trinitarian Bible Society was very near to his heart for two main reasons; he loved his Bible in the authorised version which he had used from childhood, and he longed that others might know the blessing he had received through it. On a number of occasions he spoke for the society, and with his own church gave generous support to the worldwide distribution of the Holy Scriptures.

His concern for the elderly and afflicted was seen in his support for homes for the elderly through the Aged Pilgrims' Friend Society, the Gospel Standard Bethesda Homes and, latterly, the Cherith Trust.

As an older pastor he had a very real concern for younger men in the ministry taking to heart Paul's injunction to Timothy, "And the things that thou hast heard among many witnesses, the same commit thou to faithful men, who shall be able to teach others also". This practical concern was expressed in a constant interest in the Strict Baptist Ministers' Help Society, of which he was a founder member in 1922 and of which he eventually became the President. However, his influence was not merely official but deeply personal, and many younger men, struggling with the problems of pastoral care found him a ready listener and a wise adviser. In his journeys throughout the country he said that his own spirit was refreshed by his conversation with pastors of many churches, but only the Lord knows how many of these younger men found a new stimulation and a new zeal to preach the word and to press on in spite of difficulties after conversation with this man of such patriarchal appearance, and balanced judgment.

One morning he felt constrained to phone another local pastor somewhat younger. It transpired that the younger man was seriously contemplating giving up; Mr. Delves was enabled to encourage him, and comfort him with the comfort by which he himself had often been comforted of God.

Sometimes after a spell of discouragement even he would be tempted to resign the pastorate — the word would come to mind, "Ye have dwelt long enough in this mount"; but it would fade as he felt renewed strength from the Lord, and just as before, he would be enabled to "hold on his way".

☆ ☆ ☆ ☆ ☆

His grandaughter writes feelingly of her Grandad's way of life, wide interests, and amazing knowledge:

Grandad was a very striking figure and very easily recognisable, of course. But he was always delighted to be recognised in the street by the people in Crowborough village, and he would always tell us with a little chuckle if he overheard people in the street point him out as a 'striking old gentleman'. I think he may have felt it ironic that he, who was so retiring by nature, should be so easily distinguishable in a crowd and such a focal point of interest.

He was always insistent on walking as much as possible and would often refuse to be driven. This was not altogether surprising when he was offered a ride in a 'Mini' as he had to squeeze himself up like a concertina in order to get in.

When staying with us for a break he would often browse round the library until lunch-time, dipping into various books and finally choosing two or three to bring home, which he would read in the afternoon. I wish I could remember all the books he brought back with him, because a list of them would show what really wide-ranging interests he had. However, it is not difficult for me to pick the subject which occurred most frequently i.e. Henry VIII, the later Georges and Queen Victoria. However, he would shake his head over Edward VIII. He found the reign of Henry VIII fascinating basically because of the great religious changes which had occurred and would often mention William Tyndale's prayer at the stake "Lord, open the King of England's eyes", which was so miraculously answered a few years later by Henry's break with Rome and by the Bible being made available to the common people. Because of this interest, he would visit Hampton Court, which is quite near our home, at least once every time he came to see us. He went even more often when he was on the blind register and so was entitled to free admission.

He was very impatient of any inaccuracy in these historical books; being so well versed in the subject which interested him, he could spot an inaccuracy at once and I have often thought he wanted to pass this information on to the author. He certainly let the rest of the family know when he found a mistake.

Any books on Israel or biographies of great Jewish leaders caught his eye and he was very well informed on affairs in the Middle East.

He would also fall on any book which dealt with the Communist revolution in Russia and in particular with the subsequent civil war in which the White Russians were supported by British troops.

At 6 o'clock when visiting us Grandad would listen to the news and would comment on anything that interested him. He was not interested in politics, though he was interested in politicians as people. Also, he was very interested in news about the Queen and Royal Family.

Tea-time would often produce interesting discussions and one topic of conversation was the Jehovah's Witnesses — there were a group of them in Surbiton, and Grandad was rather put out when he was staying with us once as I sent them away and he would have liked to talk to them. He was well-informed about the differences between such fringe sects.

Grandad had an immense fund of stories gathered during his many years of preaching all over the country. I'm sure it was he who told us about the lady (rather impatient for the service to end) who, during the prayer, put the hands of the clock on by 15 minutes! His stories frequently raised a laugh against himself. On one occasion, Grandad was asked to start the singing. The metre was rather complicated, he had no tunebook, and the only tune which came to mind was Adoration — unfortunately unknown to the rest of the congregation, and as he had no tunebook, he could not tell them where to look for the music. He ended by singing a solo.

Another favourite topic of conversation was his boyhood in Rushlake Green. His father had been the village blacksmith and everybody knew everybody else in that small village. When he returned there towards the end of his life, he was still able to remember the names of the people who had lived round the village green. I think Grandad got completely carried back into the past on such visits to Rushlake Green, and he would forget that he did not still live in the old family house and go into the garden. On one such occasion, the owner came out and was very pleased to show him round the house. He was very pleased to see that they still had a hook in the kitchen which his father had put up for them to hang bacon on once it had been smoked.

His daughter also writes a few notes on his general character and way of life:

It is difficult when speaking of the character of another to be absolutely impartial. My father would be the first and firmest in maintaining many faults in his character and life and abhorred eulogising. I can remember quite clearly my father once saying, "When I am gone I want no memorial service and no record of my life." But this was many years ago and as increasing age brought increasing awareness of the affection and esteem in which he was held, I think this remark made years earlier was forgotten.

Humility. I think this is the outstanding feature of my father's character. I can not remember a word of pride either in public or in private in our home life. He often mourned the pride in his heart and doubtless felt it, but it was certainly never in evidence in his life or conversation. When his sight had failed as it had in 1968/70 and again at the end of his life, someone, obviously, had to read letters to him. Of course, when reading these letters, it was important to realise that reading them was an intrusion upon the privacy intended between writer and recipient, and therefore one tried to pay as little attention as possible. But many of these letters were godly and gracious indications of affection and esteem. Father's usual comment at the end of a letter would be one of appreciation of something in the writer and he would say "You know, Chris, I can't see what it is in me that calls for this affection and esteem." He might add sometimes words to the effect "But it is very encouraging, isn't it, to think that my ministry is made so profitable".

The Jubilee services were an outstanding occasion, enjoyed and remembered by so very many and, of course, still read about in the commemorative booklet. But Father's reaction at the end of it all was expressed in the words I had heard several times before "You know, Chris, I really can't see what it is in me to bring out so much love and esteem."

Nervousness and lack of confidence. Although Father often laboured the point of his extreme nervousness, I do not think it was really appreciated or believed. One would have thought that after his long experience of speaking, even if he had been so nervous at the beginning of his ministry, his confidence would have increased and nervous tensions lessened. Perhaps to a certain extent they did, but if so, then his nervousness at the beginning of his ministerial career must have been excruciating. He has told us since of his first visit to a chapel with a large congregation when he really felt tempted to leave the vestry and run away, but the thought of meeting the assembling congregation in his flight was the only thing that stopped him. One would feel that the power of God which so clothed his ministry and maintained him for so long, also enabled him to stand before the congregation and appear (usually) as relaxed and as confident as he did.

In the main he seemed to me to be more at ease when preaching away from Forest Fold; and certainly Sunday mornings at home, prior to the service, were often times of great tension. Irritation with small matters was an obvious sequel to this strain. That he would appear within so short a time in the pulpit usually looking relaxed and confident was a weekly demonstration of a power quite beyond any human ability. I can recall a Sunday, probably about 1971 when Father was pacing up and down the bedroom saying 'Christine, I can't go through with it', but there never was a time when this fear actually prevented him from preaching.

That he was often in demand for special occasions is its own tribute to his ability to speak suitably, and he laboured hard beforehand that his subject should be profitable and appear fresh to his hearers. It is hard to believe that before giving his last wedding address of fatherly affection and pastoral wisdom he was so tortured with the feeling of inadequacy that he said he would never give another wedding address as long as he lived.

Humour. Father's humour is absolutely impossible to reproduce. He was not a "funny" man, did not tell funny stories and abhorred practical jokes. He was very suspicious of humour in the pulpit and felt that the ministry was not made more profitable by the laughing of the congregation. In any description of his character, it would appear that, at every turn, he lacked humour. And yet, humour was an undertone of his life, just below the surface, ready to appear in a warm and natural way, never directed unkindly and usually pointed against himself. He would tell of the lady who had come to him after a service saying, "I thought it was SO wonderful", here Father waited, as he laughingly described it, for some great personal compliment or acknowledgment of profit but she continued "that you could preach FOR SO LONG without any notes!"

He was an excellent raconteur and mimic which, with his kindly disposition, probably explained why he could hold children (including his own, when young) enthralled. Even his story of the man who was crossing the field and told by the farmer "That is not the way," who answered, "You don't know where I am going, so how do you know it is not the way" became unbelievably exciting and very long with various embellishments and extensions, including a blood-curdling "Hi" from the farmer.

When we were young, Friday night was bath night and afterwards Father used to cuddle us up in his arms, cut our nails (like Nebuchadnezzar's bird's claws, he often used to tell us, and a bit more about Nebuchadnezzar too sometimes) and tell us stories. I always preferred the story of our cousin Kate falling into the pond when she stayed with the Delves family at Rushlake Green. I can still remember the delicious squelching noise Father produced as the bedraggled Kate wended her way to their home with the water oozing out of her boots and the horrified reaction of their mother when she found such a pitiful child on her doorstep. Her gasp of horror and surprise still sends cold shivers down my spine!

Dislike of complaining. There were two things Father could not tolerate. One was extravagance and ostentation, and the other was a complaining spirit. He was not unsympathetic, in fact, quite the opposite and always caring for those in need, trouble or distress; in whose interests he would use any means within his power to bring relief relevant to the need. But a spirit of chronic complaint, as opposed to a spirit of thankfulness, he found very trying. Corporal punishment was only occasionally meted out to me, and the only cause I can remember was for complaining about a meal.

Dislike of change and challenge. Although within himself Father was conservative (I do not mean politically — his views were kept to himself as he felt that his position did not warrant the expression of political opinions as such) and was suspicious of change, yet in some ways he coped surprisingly well in the time in which he lived, which saw perhaps more change in every way than at any other time in history.

Challenge was something which (like visiting) Father felt unable to face and inadequate to meet, which was a great pity. Only his conscientiousness (I think) prevented him turning tail. To many of us he seemed to have tact, ability, wisdom and skill not only to meet challenges, but positively to go out and look for them. But we could not force him into a mould of our making, however well we might think the style would suit him and however much more useful and profitable we might think he could be. His extreme conscientiousness would never allow him to avoid challenge if he felt his way led to it. But his lack of confidence would prevent him from seeking it.

Willingness to learn. As mentioned earlier, Father had very little formal education; in today's terms it would be thought almost negligible. And apparently he did not seem particularly to have enjoyed school or to have shown any great promise. His great and extensive knowledge was partly the result of avid reading, a remarkable memory and a reasoning mind. It was also due to the fact that he never considered himself above instruction and also that he enjoyed discussion (*never argument* — this he considered most unprofitable) with those who did not share his viewpoint on matters, but whose opinions he was always ready to listen to and consider.

Our Mother had been educated to a greater extent than Father and it was a cause of great satisfaction to her that in that way, especially in the early days in the ministry and pastorate, she was able to help him in many ways to improve his English particularly and general knowledge and appreciation. Though very fond of poetry herself, and also literature in general, she never managed to convey that interest to Father. His reading was dedicated wholly and entirely to subject matter which interested him, rather than literature for its own sake. Even in old age, Father would never resent constructive comment on where we thought improvement might be made in various areas! Mother worked hard on improving his spelling, but not with quite the same success as in the other spheres. She always vetted his letters for him.

I think my father's personal bearing can easily and quite comprehensively be summed up in a verse from scripture "Let your moderation be known unto all men. The Lord is at hand" (Philippians 4.5).He really did live with "The Lord is at hand". Also perhaps by reason of natural disposition, tempered with grace and fostered by a life of study of the exhortations of scripture, his life and behaviour was not only one of moderation, but he had a distaste of extremes, whether in daily matters, conversation, attitudes or spiritual things.

Conversation. I can remember very clearly being reprimanded for coming home one day saying "I am dying for a cup of tea". It was pointed out, *very quietly and most firmly* that I was not in such a state, was not ever likely to be and that such language ill-fitted the situation in which I was. I have never forgotten it and think that although at the time I considered such a reproof uncalled for and somewhat pedantic, yet I have seen since, how much of our speech is in unnecessarily extreme language.

Daily Life. His general way of life was moderation. Ostentation and extravagance in any form he abhorred. Those of us who would have been better pleased to have seen his life style more befitting his position and more reflecting the esteem in which he was held by many, felt this most frustrating. A smarter house, better clothes and a larger car (in the days when he was driving) seemed much more in keeping with what might be expected for himself and for the family of a pastor and minister who had been so blessed in his church and in his wider ministry also. But the proposition of such plans gave no satisfaction to him, only displeasure and irritation.

It is a very small point, but nevertheless characteristic, that in his choice of a newspaper he would not have one with loud and sensational headlines or that form of reporting. He wanted the news, reported as quietly and factually as possible and was usually sufficiently informed and astute in those subjects which interested him, to be able to discern between truth and exaggerated journalism.

His own attitude was always one of moderation, but it was never one of "sitting on the fence". He based his principles on the scriptures, and explained clearly and logically his reasons for whatever was in question and was not to be swayed by argument, persuasions or personality. But based on scripture, these principles were always moderate in nature. Perhaps the wide appeal of his ministry and person to so many sections of the Denomination was because in him, many who held extreme views of one sort or another, could all find a mutual appreciation.

Possibly because of his long residence in the area and his outstanding figure, he was regarded with a great deal of respect by the people of Crowborough, and around. He was known to be kind, dependable and helpful. He very much appreciated this, partly because he was always anxious that whatever centred on Forest Fold should do nothing to bring the gospel preached there into disrepute. He was sensitive to the feelings and needs of neighbours and others around. Because of his particularly acute hearing, he was a great deal more aware of things going on than most people realised. He recalled with great delight, when working in Mr. Butler's grocer's shop during the war (which I believe he very much enjoyed) hearing a lady say as he was going to the counter "Oh, good, we are going to have that nice man serve us". But I do not think he appreciated this as a personal compliment so much as the feeling that it threw a little light on how a Christian should behave.

He viewed extreme attitudes and intolerance in others with sadness, sometimes tinged with a little wry humour as he shared confidences, affection and fellowship with those who held almost opposite views on some matters.

Perhaps I could mention Father's outstanding memory in this connection. His mind was almost computer-like and he was rarely wrong. That is as far as things interested him or his conscientiousness dictated that he should put his mind to them. Matters of little interest or, to him, slight importance, were easily forgotten. He worked hard at remembering people's names, family connections, interests and often their pets and neighbours too. It has been mentioned already that, while his eyesight was too poor to allow him to read, prior to cataract operations in 1970, he was able to carry through a marriage service by memory and during one time in hospital, was able to remember the whole of the epistle to the Philippians.

I recall one occasion when I had been on holiday and heard a sermon preached which I thought was quite outstanding and impressive, especially as the minister was quite young. On telling Father about it, I was astounded when he said "That was preached before by Mr....." and quickly took the relevant book from the *very many* on his shelves and turned to the sermon where I found it set out there, exactly as I had heard it preached!

With his large library, he was always rather sensitive about seeing visitors in his study. There were two reasons for this. He collected books; some of them expressing views with which he did not agree, but he felt it was incumbent upon him to be well read and informed on relevant subjects. However, he was a little anxious lest it should be thought that he endorsed and approved all books and opinions evident in the written works in which his study abounded.

Also he was afraid that people seeing so many books, and particularly so many sermons, lining his study walls, might imagine that he merely preached what he read instead of meditating and seeking to speak the word of God as revealed to him. These fears may seem a little unnecessary and exaggerated, but they were real to him and he was always anxious not to be a stumbling-block to the people of God, nor to bring the ministry into any disrepute, however slight.

Dislike of sermons recorded in shorthand. Very many people will be aware of this particular foible. It did not stem from a lack of concern for the word to be spread and for the profit to be extended, but to his intense distaste for what he knew would always follow when he saw his sermons being "taken down". "I know", he would say, "when I see someone writing shorthand, in a few days' time the envelope will come dropping through my letter-box with a typed manuscript for me to correct and this I simply cannot do". In the days of our youth, we were usually forewarned by mother to "keep clear" when sermons for revision appeared. The only time I have ever seen my father in anything like a temper was on such an occasion when he threw the type-written pages across the room and said if his preaching was sounding so ungrammatical and at times not even making sense, then something was very wrong. The only way he could correct it would be to sit down and re-write the whole thing and that was impossible. So usually it was stuffed into a corner and, hopefully, forgotten. When, therefore, he was aware that his sermons were being recorded in this way, he then found himself thinking more of their grammatical quality and how they would "read", rather than on the effect of the word on the hearts of the hearers to whom it was aimed. This distraction was most unwelcome to him.

Although initially Father did not welcome the idea of cassette tape recording of sermons, yet when his own eyesight was so poor and he could not read, he found this form of ministry a great benefit and revised his own previous antipathy to some extent. He also found that with the advent of tape-recording, shorthand and the hated sermon revision became much less in evidence and of that, at least, he approved.

☆ ☆ ☆ ☆ ☆

An old friend at Forest Fold has also given a sidelight on the deep spiritual exercises of this man of God:

Our late dear Pastor did not often speak of his spiritual experiences in private, but I remember on one occasion, he had been to our home to dinner, and instead of going straight home as he usually did, he went over to the sofa, and sat with his head in his hands looking very distressed. He said he had (in some particular way) sinned against the Lord and caused Him to hide His face from him and everything was black darkness. He wondered if he would ever be able to preach again. We tried to comfort him and reminded him of some of the promises, such as "If we confess our sins, He is faithful and just to forgive us our sins." But he could not take any comfort and went away very distressed. He evidently continued in that state for two or three weeks and then at the Branch chapel one evening he preached from Heb. 12.5-6 "My son, despise not thou the chastening of the Lord, nor faint when thou art rebuked of him: For whom the Lord loveth he chasteneth, and scourgeth every son whom he receiveth." He said it had been spoken to him, after a period of great darkness, and that the words, "My son" came with such sweetness as completely to soften and break down his spirit before the Lord - he felt if he was a son, he could willingly accept His chastening. I wish I could remember more, but that has always remained very vivid as I had privately witnessed his distress.

☆ ☆ ☆ ☆ ☆ ☆

The following is a loving testimony to both the man and his ministry by one of his older ministerial friends, Mr. G.J. Collier, Pastor of the Strict Baptist Chapel in Linslade:

God gives to each generation an outstanding instrument, by whom, in one way or another a rich crop of spiritual blessing is bestowed upon the Church. Such an instrument was Stanley Delves. It is a common feature with those whom God uses most, that they seek no glory for themselves, and although the work which God commands is substantial in its effects, they are amazed at the significance attaching to it. Such was the case with our friend; people who came into his company could not fail to recognise his spiritual stature as a minister of the Gospel and, as such, his labours carried an authority and an influence which extended far beyond his own sphere of operation, and yet were always marked by a gentleness of personality, and a most tender sympathetic spirit. His usefulness in the service of his Divine Master was extensive beyond the average, and it will be a long time before the likes of him will be seen again.

He and I spent four days together every year since 1955, with one or perhaps two exceptions. These much valued seasons, which we recognised as a kind of a 'Pocket Geneva' without opposition, were as much valued by him as they were to me. We understood each other, and it was always with a sense of loss when at the railway station, the tall stately figure waved an affectionate farewell. Once on these annual visits another minister called to break his journey for refreshment and rest, and before resuming his journey retired to the front room for a little sleep. Not wishing to disturb him, Mr. Delves went out for a short walk, returning to look through the window to see whether the sleeper had awakened, but as there seemed to be no stirring the performance was repeated once or twice more, when a phone call from a nervous neighbour declared anxiously that there was a strange man dressed in black, with a long white beard, who kept peering through the front window, and looked like a Russian spy.

Our congregation at Linslade had much cause to remember our friend's ministry, especially his visit in 1976 when two were brought to put on Christ in an open profession. There was an unusual power in the ministry that day. His concluding remarks in the evening sermon, had such telling effect, that one who had anxiously waited for something from the Lord, and was fearful that the sermon would end and leave her with nothing, received a confirming seal in the last sentences: "Someone may say; Here's my heart, Lord, take and seal it; seal it from thy courts above. Amen" Before he left at the end of the week, he had the pleasure of hearing from this person what her experience had been under the Word.

Like the Apostle Paul, Mr. Delves needed no letters of commendation, he shunned advertisement and scorned self-praise, mere publicity was an abomination, yet he could not be hid; the honours that come from the Lord will make a man conspicuous. Those who were his spiritual hearers found his ministry was so well balanced with expository and experimental teaching, drawn at all times from the Word of Truth itself. I remember when at school a master used to demand that a straight line should be drawn freehand which when completed, he would place a ruler alongside, revealing the defects and imperfection of the effort. This was my experience in hearing our friend preach. His preaching was a model. He ever sought to present Christ in the Gospel, and he longed after the souls of poor and needy sinners that they might behold savingly the glory of the Lord.

His last visit to us here, and his last letter to me will stand out as amongst the choicest memories in our relationship with him. Taking a cup of tea into his room on the last morning of his last visit, I was relating an incident that had taken place with a grandchild, which so amused him, that he put his heart tablet, that he was about to take, into his cup of tea instead of his mouth. He was very human, and so fond of children, and they of him.

His last letter dated 30 January 1978 conveyed the sad tidings that he would not be able to come for the Anniversary, saying: 'My personal affection for you prompts me to write this personal letter.....I cling to Jesus Christ. You know that I have met with much acceptance in the ministry, and I hope not without profit, but it does not now give me a straw to cling to. It may be the Lord's will to restore me somewhat, in which case we may meet again, but if not I know that I shall die with your affection' Yes indeed! We felt a real love to each other in life, and his memory remains as a sacred treasure.

Such then is a simple but inadequate portrait of a man greatly beloved, a man who could say with the Psalmist, "Truly I am thy servant", and was surely "lovely and pleasant" in his life.

10

At Evening Time

"But it shall be one day which shall be known to the LORD, not day, not
night: but it shall come to pass, that at evening time it shall be light"

Zechariah 14.7.

There is a peculiar beauty and peace in the calm of a summer
evening as the sun leaves the sky gloriously tinted with the promise
of another day, a day of sunshine without clouds. Life with all its
bustle and noise is slowly silenced and the hearts of many are
affected by a new sense of quietness, easing away the strain of their
busy lives and preparing them for the needful refreshment of sleep.
So surely, there is a peculiar beauty in the end of a believer's
life as God most graciously and tenderly prepares His children for
sleep, as He encourages them to leave behind the sorrows and
tribulations, the perplexities and responsibilities, the relationships
and loves of their long life of obedience and service. Eminently this
was true for this dear man of God. Many had been the times when
the certainty of death had faced him and when, by the grace of God,
he had come safely through the "Valley of the shadow." A "good
hope through grace" had sustained his fainting spirit and a merciful
God had given him foretastes of glory.

Some evidence of the way in which the Lord was directing his
mind towards the great truth of the end of all things was evident in
March 1976 when visiting Tamworth Road Chapel, Croydon. He
read from 2 Peter 1 and 3, two very solemn chapters about the
second coming of Christ. After finishing the reading, he started to
pray but his voice got slower and quieter and finally ceased. The
alarmed congregation waited fearfully, unsure what to do as he
appeared to have fainted. A few moments later he recovered and
continued in prayer in a weak voice but coherently. At the conclusion
he was helped out of the pulpit but after a short rest returned to
preach a short sermon from 2 Peter 3.14. With his usual courtesy
and concern he apologised for the break in the service and
continued, not mentioning his weakness. On arriving at the home of
his friends, Mrs. and Miss Miles, afterwards, he said he had no
recollection of what had occurred and recalled very little of what he
had said in prayer. It could only be concluded that he was upheld in

his spirit by the Lord although his mind and body were in an almost unconscious state. In the evening he was fully recovered and preached a powerful sermon from the same words. The circumstances and the subject made a very deep impression upon those who heard him that day.

The subject of the second coming of Christ seemed to fill his mind frequently as he drew near to death. A ministerial friend once asked him what he felt was the cause of the present decline in our churches and to his surprise the reply was, "The almost total lack of teaching about the second coming of Christ."

On his final visit to Croydon he again felt the nearness of the end and said to the deacons and Pastor at Tamworth Road, "I shall die clinging to Jesus Christ."

Years before, during one Sunday School anniversary, the hymn having been announced he stood to read the first verse or two as was the practice. Having read: "Home! home! sweet sweet home! Prepare me, dear Saviour, for yonder blest home," with much emotion, he sat down unable to go on and the superintendent had to finish announcing the hymn. Even then his eyes were looking towards the heavenly country.

His increasing weakness compelled more serious thoughts about his pastorate, thoughts which for a number of years had made him remind his people that they should be looking for his successor. It was his hope that someone could come to take his place whilst he was still there to hand on, as it were, the mantle of the pastorate. These thoughts sprang from the deep pastoral concern he felt for his flock and the desire that they would not be left without spiritual care when the time came for him to be "for ever with the Lord." When advocating this course of action he would say, "My people cannot pray me from the grave for ever."

At the commencement of 1977 he felt the time had come to resign his pastorate and as he approached his eightieth birthday his deacons were compelled to realise that his ministry was indeed coming to its close. However, the desirability of seeing a successor, and the practical matter of appointing one, were two entirely different things. The love, the relationship, and the regard his people felt for him was like the bond of a true human marriage which can never be broken but by death and so it was really only a nominal retirement. He was still his people's pastor and they were still his flock even though increasingly the services and church meetings had to be conducted by others.

The minutes of the church meeting held on 10 January 1977 state:

. Mr. Delves then announced his intention to retire at the end of this year when he will be 80. Feels preaching etc. a great strain and that he should retire before becoming too feeble. Feels he deserves a rest. Spoke of harmony in Church between Pastor and deacons and members and that his retirement is not due to any trouble in the Church. Has not come to this suddenly but we should pray for a successor. Mr. J. Fermor spoke in prayer. Mr. Delves closed with prayer.

The Pastor is concerned that we do not settle down to a supply ministry. It is desirable that a new pastor is chosen. Gracious and prayerful exercise of mind is recommended.

During the summer of 1977 a last visit was made to his friends in churches in the Midlands and it was evident that there surely could not be another such time of spiritual blessing and fellowship. He was very tired, a tiredness only really overcome in the pulpit, when the sermons preached at Leicester, Coventry and Old Hill had the same unction and power as ever. The closing months of the year evidenced increasing weakness until in December he was partially confined to his bed by the window on the ground floor of his home, facing the chapel where he could lovingly and prayerfully watch his church and congregation gathering for their meetings.

A typical message was taken from his sickroom to the people on 3 December 1977 expressing his love to them all:

My beloved friends,
Although I much dislike intruding myself into the service and worship of God, I feel I must say how deeply affected I have felt by all your love and kindness to me this week on the occasion of my 80th birthday. I very much appreciate your beautiful gifts and cards and letters. Indeed, I have felt quite overwhelmed with it all. The Lord knows how I feel, but I cannot very well express it. It is impossible for me to reply to each one personally, so I ask you to accept this expression of gratitude to you all.

I still continue extremely weak, but the matter is in the Lord's hands and I hope in due time I may be strengthened to come before you again.

I am very grateful to Mr. Kinderman for leaving his people to come to us this morning and to them for willingly agreeing to this.

With my love to you all, both young and old,

Your affectionate Pastor,

S. Delves

On another occasion he sent a message to a meeting at the chapel saying:

I am too ill to be with you all tonight. I send my love and feel I could embrace you all in a holy kiss.

A silence of painful but sacred sorrow fell on all who were present.

In the earlier part of what proved to be his last illness he said to a visiting friend, "Although not favoured at present with special blessings, I get assurance and peace from the Saviour's words 'Him that cometh to me I will in no wise cast out'. I came to Him *years* ago and I have been coming ever since. His love and His blood have been so precious to me at times that I know He has not cast me out and I feel sure He never will."

During his long life there had been times of great agitation of mind and spirit and especially during periods of weakness and pain, but now there seemed to be a deepening calm and repose. To one of his members he said, "Brother, I am dying but all is well. I have no fears, everything I preached, every truth and doctrine has been sorely tried but not now. I rest on Jesus. The things I have preached, I can not only live by but die on."

His cousins Mrs. and Miss Miles from Croydon visited him on 16 February and were much distressed to see his weak and jaundiced condition but with an effort he began to talk and said that he was perfectly peaceful in mind and body. He was surrounded with every comfort and had constant communion with the Lord. The devil was not permitted to distress him and he lived in the text, "Thou wilt keep him in perfect peace, whose mind is stayed on thee". Isaiah 26.3. He had no fear of death whatsoever. When he was so active preaching so many sermons he was often troubled because he felt he might use the Bible simply as a book of texts but he now knew this was not so because his soul was being blessed by the truth itself. He spoke of a special time in hearing Ephesians 1. read in the chapel and relayed to his bedside. He said that Mr. Philpot used to say that as he got older his religion got simpler, and he could say the same. His testimony was:

> "Jesus, thy blood and righteousness
> My beauty are, my glorious dress."

He felt sad that so many of the 'tatters' of his own righteousness still clung to him but he did not trust in them, nor in all his preaching, but only in Jesus Christ for salvation. He had been meditating on the words, "For he hath made him to be sin for us" 2 Cor. 5.21. and although he could not understand the depth of meaning in them, he believed the words were true of him.

His daughter Rachel, and sometimes visiting friends, had been reading *Pilgrim's Progress* to him in the evenings and he had been thinking especially of the passage of the pilgrim through the valley of the shadow of death. Fifty years ago he said he had passed through the valley before and it was a terrible experience (This referred to his experience when suffering from T.B. and not expecting to recover). "But", he said, smiling calmly, "This time it is different. 'I will fear no evil: for thou art with me'." Seeing that his strength was going his friends did not let him talk any more and in parting, he sent his special love to all the friends at Croydon.

It was noticeable that a change had come over the feelings of his people as this illness progressed. On so many former occasions their prayers had been urgent and fervent for his recovery, prayers which had been so wonderfully and sometimes so suddenly answered. Now the Lord took away that desire to pray for his recovery as a spirit of sad but loving submission to what was seen as the will of the Lord, was evident amongst his people.

As the month of February progressed, the news began to spread over the country amongst his many friends that the man so greatly beloved was dying. His own dear people were tearful but resigned as they came quietly to creep into his room for a last word or look from their Pastor and on the very last Lord's day of his life, at their request, all the young people of the congregation made a brief visit to his room when he was able to speak to them, remembering each one personally by name.

One of his church members recalls her feelings at the time:

The memory of our beloved Pastor is so fragrant: some of us feel that we have lost one of our dearest friends on earth.

When he was very ill, Mr. Delves said, "You won't forget your old Pastor will you?" *Forget* him! We miss his ministry so much but were thankful that our souls were fed right to the end of his life. He always wanted to speak well of his Lord and was so fearful of getting repetitive.

As I am writing this, I can hear his voice a few weeks before he died, earnestly saying: "Don't let them make too much of Stanley Delves. The cry from the bottom of my heart is -

'A guilty, weak, and helpless worm.
On thy kind arms I fall
Be Thou my strength and righteousness,
My Jesus and my all.'   *Watts*

That's all I am — a weak and helpless worm — but *HE* is all and in all."

I was favoured to be with him on several occasions when he was too weak to be alone. One cannot explain the nearness to heaven in that little room. One day he said, "I don't want to be critical of dear Rutherford because I can so understand the warmth of his spirit saying:

'And if one soul from Anwoth,
Meet me at God's right hand,
My Heaven will be two Heavens,
In Immanuel's Land',

but I cannot feel that. I feel that Heaven with Jesus Christ will be absolutely everything that my soul longs for. Perfect happiness — wonderful happiness — to be with Jesus."

Another time I was reading the whole of I Thessalonians to him, when he suddenly interrupted me and said, "Please would you mind reading it slowly: I don't want to miss even one word. There is such depth in every expression. I have never seen it quite like this before."

He said that the Epistles especially had been so good to him and none more so than the first chapter of Ephesians.

He was overwhelmed by all the letters of love and appreciation sent to him. He said, "I have many loved friends all over the country, many that I have visited year after year, and it has not been easy to tell them that I shall not be able to go any more." He dictated a few letters for me to write and I remember him particularly having a struggle in controlling himself whilst telling me what to say to a very old friend, Mr. Collier. He said, "We've had such sweet communion together and I feel this is the last good-bye on earth."

One day he had the local florist to visit him with flowers from his people, who told him that no Pastor could have had a more loving flock. Actually, the person who had ordered the flowers had already told the same man that no church could have had a more loving Pastor!

Many witnessed his quiet spirit in his illness, but one Sunday about six weeks before he died, I went in to see him after the morning service and he completely broke down and sobbed. He quickly regained his composure and said, "O you must think me a poor weak thing, but it was hard watching my beloved flock going into the House of the Lord whilst the poor under-shepherd had to stay here so helpless. I do long to come in."

Another time, he said, "Although I am supposed to have retired as your Pastor, I bear you all on my heart more than ever." I said, "You are our Pastor." He said, "Well really at the bottom of my heart, I feel I am."

He had asked us to pray for another pastor, but many of us felt that we could not pray with sincerity and feeling all the time we were being so helped under his ministry.

Of course, he was too weak to visit any of his sick people, but one of his older, loving members was ill. He gave a message on the phone, "Give her and her husband my love but if there's anything better that can express the deep feeling that I have for them at this time, then give them that." He spoke of the precious bond that is between those that love the Lord, and added, "Well, it is quite out of this world."

One morning when he was very ill, he said in a weak voice, "You know it says in the Scriptures 'My meditation of him shall be sweet.' (Psalm 104.34). Well, it really was last night. I entered so much into Gadsby's hymn 1123"

He had had that hymn read to him four times that day.

Forest Fold Chapel, Crowborough, Sussex.

Pastor Stanley Delves with his five deacons in 1974:
Standing, left to right, Ernest Constable, Ronald Bishop and
John Relf: seated, John Fermor, Pastor and Percy Barker.

The Graveyard, Forest Fold Chapel, looking toward the chapel
buildings from the site of Mr. Delves' grave.

The Headstone of the grave of Pastor and Mrs. Stanley Delves.

Stretch'd on the cross, the Saviour dies;
Hark! his expiring groans arise!
See, from his hands, his feet, his side,
Runs down the sacred crimson tide!

But life attends each deathful sound,
And flows from every bleeding wound;
The vital stream, how free it flows,
To save and cleanse his rebel foes!

To suffer in the traitor's place,
To die for man, surprising grace!
Yet pass rebellious angels by—
O why for man, dear Saviour, why?

Can I survey this scene of woe,
Where mingling grief and wonder flow?
And yet my heart unmoved remain,
Insensible to love or pain?

Come, dearest Lord, thy power impart,
To warm this cold and stupid heart;
Till all its powers and feelings move
In melting grief and ardent love.   *Steele*

I wish I could remember all he said but he had been broken down by contemplating Jesus' death. My father was present, but as he is deaf Mr. Delves said, "Now you will tell your father what a sweet night I had, won't you? and about the hymn."

He also recounted that the last Lord's Supper he was able to attend was very specially blessed to him. He felt he had had such sweet communion with his Lord. He added, "I know this was a much lower pleasure, but it was lovely to be able to sit next to Christine for the first time on such a sacred occasion."

A week before he died he could only whisper, but he said, "My dear people are all loving me into heaven." I could not reply, so he said again, "Can you hear what I'm saying? - you are all loving me into heaven: it is very sweet."

To me, the most touching time was a few days before he died when I was supporting his poor frail body in helping him to sit up. I felt broken down remembering with such thankfulness the many times the Lord had used him to support my poor frail spirit by showing me "Jesus only".

The doctor mentioned that not only had he had every care and attention from his family, but his religion was a tremendous support to him.

Two friends who had, as ministers, benefited so much from his encouragement and advice, visited him on 23 February and recorded their experiences on that memorable occasion:

On our arrival at Chapel House, Forest Fold, we were greeted by

Christine, Mr. Delves' daughter, who immediately warned us not to be surprised by how ill her father looked, and asked us not to press him with questions.

As we entered his room Christine was saying, "Here are two friends who I do not think you will want me to send away," to which, seeing us, he replied, "No, I'm *sure* I should not want them sent away." He was lying peacefully, though appearing very jaundiced. As he lay, he could see, through the window, the chapel he loved and where he had laboured so long.

We began to speak to him, and express our concern and affection for him, and then he said, "Who is this kind man they keep talking about, and coming to show their love to? — I'm sure I don't know him!" One of them replied, "You know, the sheep cannot see the mark on its own back, but others can." He smiled. He wanted to be lifted up so as to speak better, but it was impracticable.

Then he said, moistening his lips frequently, "Last night was a bad night; I usually have some of the doctor's medicine and get a good sleep, but I could not get off last night, so early in the morning I had a Disprin to ease the pain, and so it did, but I am not at my best just now — I shall be more clear-headed when I have slept off the effects. I'm afraid I hardly know what I'm saying. But I had some sweet thoughts last night from Hymn 1123 (see previous page), 'Stretched on the cross the Saviour dies.' It was a sweet touch. I do not *live* on these touches, you know — I live by faith in Jesus Christ — but it is very nice to have these thoughts. P...., you read it to me, and then D...., you pray." P...., read verses 1 and 2, and was then interrupted as the dear man repeated the words, "But life attends each deathful sound." At the end of the hymn he said, "That is real religion, isn't it, P.... You know, I think it was Philpot who once said that as he grew older, so his religion grew simpler; and that is how I find it; my religion can be summed up in this:
"Nothing in my hand I bring,
Simply to thy cross I cling".
I do not know what may happen to me, though I walk through the valley of the shadow of death, I fear no evil — and I don't. I do not know if my last days will be conscious or unconscious, whether they will be filled with joy or not, but you can tell all my friends—any of my friends—that I die 'clinging to Jesus Christ.' Now D...., please." So D.... prayed shortly, speaking of there being ten thousand instructors in Christ but not many fathers; thanking God that Mr. Delves had been a spiritual father to us, and saying that soon the day would break and the shadows would flee away.

After this Mr. Delves said, "I expect the next thing you will hear is that it's all over. I've told my people that I want them to sing that hymn at my grave as their pastor's dying testimony:
'When this poor lisping stammering tongue
Lies silent in the grave,
Then in a nobler sweeter song,
I'll sing Thy power to save'
He was evidently tired by this, and we took his hand. One said, "You know, in heaven they say, Blessing, and honour, and glory, and power be unto him that sitteth upon the throne, and unto the Lamb for ever and ever. Amen."

He replied with a smile, "Yes, that is my testimony too."

We then left to go to lunch with Mr. & Mrs. Bishop — he is one of the deacons. Their sadness was so evident, but in conversation he related what Mr. Delves had said to him a few days before, about one of his old members: "You know when Mrs. King was dying, I went to see her; and she said she had been so blessed with the thought that 'underneath are the everlasting arms;' so I said to her, 'Well, Mrs. King, all you have to do now is to leave all your cares and concerns, and lean back completely on those arms' — and that is just where I am now."

A few days before the end he was discussing the funeral service with his dear friend, David Obbard, and said, "These arrangements are very sorrowful to my family but I feel that I am just arranging my bedroom — soon I shall wake up in glory."

And so on 4 March 1978 his spirit was loosed from all that is mortal and entered into the joy of his Lord. A pastorate of fifty-four years concluded in love and thankfulness, a life of devotion to the Saviour was crowned with a peace which passes all understanding, and another faithful servant received the crown of glory from the hand of his Master.

The funeral service on 11 March was conducted by the five younger ministers who had all gone to preach with the advice and encouragement of their Pastor.

After an opening prayer by Mr Henry Godley the very large congregation sang the hymn by *Cowper*

"There is a fountain filled with blood
Drawn from Immanuel's veins,
And sinners plunged beneath that flood,
Lose all their guilty stains"

Mr. Godley then said:

It was our beloved Pastor's expressed wish that each one of his sons in the ministry should take a part in this solemn and blessed service. As my beloved Pastor said to me, and doubtless of course to others, 'I have no need to go outside. Why should I go outside? There are you five dear brethren and I want you all to take part'. And so the order of the service will be thus:
Scripture Reading, by Mr. David Crowter; prayer will be offered by Mr. John Relf; the address by Mr. Philip Kinderman; the committal will be by Mr. David Obbard.

This day is a day which many of us have anticipated with much mixed feeling in our hearts. Now that day has arrived. We have lost a beloved Pastor, one who meant so much to us for so many years. Thirty-five years ago now, almost, he baptized this poor sinner, a spiritual father, a teacher, a faithful minister of the Lord Jesus Christ. But in our sorrow it becometh us to remember those who have lost not only a Pastor, but a father, one dear to them in the flesh and in the spirit.

You may know that our beloved Pastor was given much peace of mind toward his latter end. For the last several weeks he was kept in peace. He said to me on one occasion, "I have been the subject of temptation all my life, Henry. Not a truth which I have preached but Satan has assailed it, concerning its truth and veracity. But now there is not a shadow of temptation. It is all peace. I'm a great sinner and I cannot know or see all my sin. God's eyes are holy and penetrating; He knows them all. But I rest my soul secure upon the righteousness and blood and obedience of the Lord Jesus Christ. I stand complete and faultless in Him." Wonderful words! They were from the mouth of one who by the grace and Spirit of God has been enabled for so many years — 54 years here as Pastor and a few years longer of course in the whole of his ministry — faithfully, tenderly and lovingly to preach a precious Christ and to warn everyone. His ministry was made solemn and deep and searching by the Holy Spirit.

I feel I may speak for my beloved brethren. We are each one of us quite happy and contented to do that which has been asked of us. We do not vie with one another; we pray earnestly and lovingly one for the other, and we esteem it a great privilege and an honour and a blessing to pay our last respects to our beloved Pastor in this manner. And just a personal word: it is a favour, an honour, a privilege, a blessing that I never once thought would come my way. The Lord help our beloved brethren."

Mr. David Crowter then read Revelation 7. 9-17, 14. 1-5, 12-13. and 21.1-7, Mr. John Relf then prayed with deep feeling, after which Mr. Philip Kinderman spoke.

My beloved friends, it is my privilege and my responsibility to speak a few words to your hearts this afternoon. And I do so on behalf of the family and our people at Forest Fold here. I do not feel to speak only for myself, though I must speak in a personal way, and you will expect me to do so. It is a concern and a desire with me to speak that which is good and right in the sight of our God.

The presence of so many friends from so many places far and near shows that great regard in which our Pastor was held. It is overwhelming to us to see it and to feel that spirit of affection which was so widespread, so justly his portion. We remember that many places have, with us, lost a faithful minister, a man of God, a fervent and able preacher of the Gospel, and a tender friend, a particular friend to so many. But you will remember too that we have lost more - we have lost a father. We have lost a beloved and faithful pastor, one who was especially dear. And this is something that cannot be replaced, indeed we do not expect it. As I anticipated this day and this occasion, I had mixed feelings of thankfulness with a sense of grievous loss. The loss is great, we can hardly realise it yet. But there is thankfulness that he died as he lived. And he died as he wished, surrounded by the affection of his own people, amidst them, in the quietness of his home with his family. And he died in the fulness of the peace of the gospel, and in that which he so long preached as the foundation of his hope and the hope of every poor sinner, in the Lord Jesus Christ. I remember him speaking on one occasion so solemnly, so forcefully and yet so blessedly of what we need; that wedding garment, the righteousness of Christ imputed and the spirit of Christ imparted. How true! And in that confidence, and in that spirit he ended his days.

It was with a sense of thankfulness that we saw him in his last days. The Lord so gently and so mercifully brought him to his end on earth that it was a blessing to be with him. Many will testify that they felt it to be a privilege to enter into his presence, to feel his affection, to have that sense of the Lord's rich peace resting upon him and to feel that the gospel that he preached was indeed his support to the end of this mortal life. It is hard to realise the loss. Hard to realise yet that he will not, as before, return again from the borders of the grave. I think back on those times when we saw him in hospital, and times of course, before my recollection when he was grievously ill, when the Lord so wonderfully restored him and brought him back to his people enabling him again to preach the word with vigour and effect.

We thank God today for remarkable things, and remember the mercy, the times of trouble, of affliction and of deliverance and return. But we cannot and do not expect that life here can go on for ever, nor of course, was it his desire or his wish in the weariness of life, in the infirmity and illness of latter days. How he longed, as he would have us to long, to be with Christ which is far better. How he always, in the ministry of the word, put this as the end and the aim of every true believer, to win Christ, using those words of the Apostle Paul — "That I may win Christ and be found in him". How he would insist that this is the end, the aim, the goal. Not just to listen to beautiful sermons, though that is good and profitable for us. Not just to be in the fellowship of the Lord's people, though we have enjoyed that and I emphasize how we have enjoyed that and realised the heavenly sense of it, but beyond that, O! far above, is the glory that he has entered into by the mercy of the Lord. And he would say to us, as often he has said, that it is only by the mercy of the Lord. It is not because he preached for so long — that is a very remarkable thing and we remember and remark on it, it is an extraordinary thing, but not just for that, not only because of his godly life. The godly life was the effect of the grace of God and demonstration of that spirit of Christ which dwelt in him, but as he would say to us, "It is by the mercy of the Lord". I remember him speaking to me, so typically in the early days of my ministry, enquiring how I felt. I said, "I wish I had more ability". "Ah", he said to me, "Philip, I used to wish that I had more ability but I wish now that I had more grace". And he did not mean it as a reproof but it came to me with such an emphasis and a tenderness, it was typical of his spirit, that he could say to me, "we need more grace". That is what we need, and how vital that we enter into heaven by the blood of Jesus Christ. Again he said to me on one occasion, "People say to me, 'When you come to the end, surely you will hear the voice of the Lord saying "Well done, good and faithful servant.' But", he said, "I don't look for that you know, I look to enter into heaven, by the mercy of the Lord Jesus Christ." And that is good. No doubt he has experienced that reception, no doubt his works do follow him. We are agreed that he was a good and faithful servant.

I do not feel that I can, nor is it the occasion to try, to enter into any life history, nor am I desirious or able to preach a sermon to you upon death or the end, but I do feel that I want to just put before you these thoughts that the life of our dear pastor is to us an example and an encouragement. It is both of these. An example and an encouragement. And there is cause for thankfulness and encouragement. For consider that ministry of the Word which he maintained so long by the Lord's grace. It is an example to us. It is an example to the many ministers who are gathered here with me. We are not all like him. We cannot all minister for so many years. We shall not all be pastors for that great span. We shall not all, of course, have those same abilities. We shall not all have such an extensive ministry. But he was an example to us, for truly it is to be said that as he taught and preached Jesus Christ the words were true of him, as Paul could say, that he was the servant of the churches. "For we preach not ourselves, but Christ Jesus the Lord".

"Remember," says the apostle to the Hebrews in that thirteenth chapter, "Remember them which have the rule over you, who have spoken unto you the word of God: whose faith follow, considering the end of their conversation. Jesus Christ the same yesterday, and today, and forever." Remembering and considering their faith. It is his faith that we are to follow, and that end of the ministry.

How humble he was and how nervous. How he felt his own inabilities. How he regarded himself as but an instrument of the Lord. And there are several here who remember with vividness no doubt, his coming to Forest Fold. He has spoken of it to me and how he felt overwhelmed with that responsibility and how as he graphically put it, when he attempted to preach here at first, he felt finished before he had begun. But the Lord sustained him, supported him, gave him fresh grace, fresh ability and fresh oil to anoint him. This is an example and an encouragement to us. An encouragement that the gospel continues and the fulness of it is ever there in Christ Jesus our Lord and we draw from that fulness. I remember over 20 years ago when I was in the army, men saying to me, "Well where do you go?" And as I spoke of the ministry they wondered that a man could be there for 30 years and still preach the same things. "How monotonous", they thought, "surely he must have run out of sermons", but you know how the Lord so wonderfully provided, and how the ministry was fresh, fresh until his very end. And so this is an encouragement to us. It is an example to us all as believers. It is right that we should speak to his honour. It is right that his memory is so blessed, and will be.

It is good that we should say that his life was upright, eminently so, that his way was gracious and so loving. He deeply felt the truth of what he so often put before us in the preaching of the word, that the gospel is for sinners indeed and the blood of Jesus Christ is so absolutely essential to cleanse our hearts. You must not think that a man of God, so eminent and used had a different foundation for his faith, or that God received him on different terms, not at all.

No doubt it cannot be the same here at Forest Fold. No question but that we feel that great loss and great difference, but thankfully we do not say that it is the end of the gospel of Christ, nor the collapse of his Church. You will remember that it would be quite contrary to everything he has preached and stood for to suggest that our spiritual lives would be at an end, or that we should have no comfort and consolation because our dear pastor has been taken.

Now let me just say these two things. I did feel that he was always so faithful as well as affectionate in the ministry of the word. The two were so bound together. As I first came here, I found his ministry so searching and I came to realise it was so because it was so faithful and so loving. His words went home because there was a love for souls, and a concern above all for their eternal welfare. What he was as a minister he was as a man. In his home and in all his relations he was the same; faithful, and affectionate, so very gracious and benevolent and yet so commanding in a gracious way.

What a loss this is in his home. For the ministry of the word he gave up much. Because of the ministry of the word and because he was the pastor of this church his family faced many demands upon it. Yet the Lord has graciously supplied them with strength and we believe that He will do so. I yet feel that it is right simply and sincerely to say that the ministry that has been known among the churches is as much his testimony as anything else. Although he has been taken and no more shall we see his kindly face, and hear his faithful words in person, and know his commanding and authoritative and yet so gracious presence, yet we pray it may be that what he has commenced shall continue and the work that he has begun so prayerfully, the Lord will maintain and prosper. May He bless you each this afternoon and in the time to come.

The congregation then sang a hymn which had also been sung at the funeral of Mrs. Delves, fifteen years before,

"Blessed are they whose guilt is gone,
Whose sins are washed away with blood,
Whose hope is fixed on Christ alone,
Whom Christ has reconciled to God"   *Hart*

Like Stephen, devout men carried him to his burial. He was laid beside his dear wife and not far from his little boy and then Mr. David Obbard spoke:

As it hath pleased Almighty God to call hence the soul of our dear brother here departed, we commit his body to the ground, earth to earth, ashes to ashes, dust to dust, in sure and certain hope of resurrection to eternal life through our Lord Jesus Christ, who shall change our vile body, that it may be fashioned like unto His glorious body, according to the working whereby He is able even to subdue all things unto Himself.

How often have these words been uttered by our Pastor as he has stood by the grave of others, and now he has come to his end. How long will it be before other voices utter them beside ours? It is a good spiritual exercise to ask ourselves the question, "When my body lies here, where will my soul be?" The voice of our Pastor is silent, but he speaks to you today. He said to me, "David, do not eulogise me, but tell the people the truths that I have preached are truths to live by and to die by." That voice comes to you, as it were, from beyond the grave today, "The truths that I have preached are truths to live by and die by." Let us now hear the Word of God.

1 Corinthians 15. 51-57 was then read, and Mr. Obbard
continued:

Dear friends, we lay in the grave today the mortal remains of our beloved
Pastor. As has been said already, a counsellor, a friend, a guide, and many
of us can say, a father. For I am sure that there are hundreds, not only here
at Forest Fold but throughout this land, to whom he could say as Paul to the
Corinthians, "Though ye have ten thousand instructors in Christ, yet have
ye not many fathers." (1 Cor. 4.15). He was our father; we loved him and
he loved us, in Christ. Not only do we lay here the remains of our father,
spiritually, but also we lay here a 'Mr. Valiant-for-truth'. And I feel moved to
read to you the account of the passing of Bunyan's Mr. Valiant-for-truth:

"After this it was noised abroad that Mr. Valiant-for-truth was taken by a
summons, by the same post as the other, and had this for a token that this
summons was true, that his pitcher was broken at the fountain. When he
understood it, he called for his friends and told them of it. Then said he, 'I am
going to my Father's, but with great difficulty I got hither. Yet now I do not
repent me of all the trouble that I have been to, to arrive where I am. My
sword I give to him that shall succeed me on my pilgrimage, and my courage
and skill to him that can get it. My marks and scars I carry with me to be a
witness for me that I have fought His battles who will now be my Rewarder'
When the day that he must go hence was come, many accompanied him to
the river-side, into which, as he went, he said, 'Death, where is thy sting?'
And as he went deeper he said, 'Grave, where is thy victory?' So he passed
over, and the trumpets sounded for him on the other side."

Though we mourn, yet there is that note of victory. I thought how paralleled
in our Pastor's last days were the experiences of Mr. Valiant-for-truth.
How, as he began to go down into the river, he said, "Death, where is thy
sting?" For the sting of death is sin and our sin has been removed by the
Saviour who bore it for us. Our pastor said to me a few days before he
passed on. "Rachel has been reading to me from Pilgrim's Progress; the
valley of the Shadow of Death with all its noise and its fears and its
hobgoblins. But, David, there are no hobgoblins here. All is peace. All is
quietness. I am proving the fulfilment of God's promise, 'Thou wilt keep him
in perfect peace whose mind is stayed on Thee'." As he went down deeper,
"O grave where is thy victory?" My friends, we are used to seeing graves
opened and filled, but do we realise the wonder of this, that one day these
graves will be opened and emptied? What a shout there will be! What a
shout from this hallowed spot! My father lies here; my grandfather lies here;
my great grandfather lies here. There are many here who will rise in that
day. Remember the words of Job: "All the days of my appointed time will I
wait till my change come. Thou shalt call, and I will answer." (Job 14:
14-15). Paul says that the Lord will come from heaven with the voice of the
archangel and with the trump of God. And the dead in Christ shall rise first
(1 Thes. 4.16) "O grave, where is thy victory? Thanks be unto God which
giveth us the victory through our Lord Jesus Christ."

Let us not be ashamed of our tears today, but through our tears let us
raise our song of victory to the Lord Jesus Christ, who gives us victory, not

only in this life, as He gave it to our Pastor, but in death and beyond the grave.

> "Lo, Jesus greets us, risen from the tomb;
> Lovingly He meets us, scattering fear and gloom;
> Thine be the glory, risen, conquering Son;
> Endless is the victory Thou for us hast won."

O! let that note be in our hearts this afternoon as we stand here. An endless victory Christ our Saviour has bought for us. And so it is with sadness, and yet it is with humble thankfulness that we gather here.

> "And when my latest breath,
> Shall rend this veil in twain;
> Through death I shall escape from death,
> And life eternal gain."

May that be our experience, and now may we join together in prayer, as we would praise our God and thank Him for His grace in Jesus Christ.

Over six hundred friends who had gathered from all over the country stood in silent prayer and meditation, then passed slowly by the open, eloquent, grave to leave the mortal remains of a "prince and a great man" in the peace of Forest Fold graveyard but a few yards from the pulpit where for so long he proclaimed the Gospel of Christ. The mixed sorrow and thanksgiving of the day was shared by many hundreds more unable to be there and from many hearts flowed praise to God for such a testimony.

"And one of the elders answered, saying unto me, What are these which are arrayed in white robes? and whence came they? And I said unto him, Sir, thou knowest. And he said to me, These are they which came out of great tribulation, and have washed their robes, and made them white in the blood of the lamb. Therefore are they before the throne of God, and serve him day and night in his temple: and he that sitteth on the throne shall dwell among them."

Revelation 7.14-15.

143

11

Their Works Do Follow Them

"And I heard a voice from heaven saying unto me, Write, Blessed are the dead which die in the Lord from henceforth: Yea, saith the Spirit, that they may rest from their labours; and their works do follow them"

Revelation 14.13.

From so long and fruitful a life it has been a most difficult task to select sermons and writings which would help to give a picture of Mr. Delves' ministry. The printed page can never fully express the warmth and varied emphases of the spoken word nor can the formality of a printed sermon convey the heart warming spirituality of his preaching.

In the kind providence of God, handwritten notes of his first sermon were found after his death and from a tape recording we have a complete transcript of his final message to his own people. The sermon preached on the death of the former pastor at Forest Fold, when Mr. Delves was but twenty three years old is printed because it expresses so much that must be said of his own life and testimony and also because its closing prayer has been so completely answered. The notes of the sermon, *"The Preaching of the Cross"*, again found after his death, but written early in his ministry, give a vivid outline of his convictions regarding what was to be his life's work.

THE TABERNACLE OF GOD IS WITH MEN.

"And I heard a great voice out of heaven saying, Behold, the tabernacle of God is with men, and he will dwell with them, and they shall be his people, and God himself shall be with them, and be their God."

Revelation 21.3. *

These words and their context contain the accomplishment of God's purpose from before the foundation of the world, and the final overthrow of the plans of Satan begun in the Garden of Eden. Adam, created in the image of God, lived in friendship and communion with Him. Satan, whose purpose it was to destroy mankind, by temptation caused Adam to fall, and

*This is a transcript of handwritten notes by Mr. Deves and although dated 15.8.19 was evidently the substance of his first sermon preached at the Little Dicker chapel on 2 November 1919, see page 24.

thereby apparently attained his purpose, namely that man should be separated from God. God, by His promise there, declared that Satan's design should be doomed to failure, and this text in the end of the Bible is the ultimate fulfilment of that promise that man should again dwell in peace with God.

God dwelt with men in His tabernacle according to His promise to Moses in giving the instructions for its erection and furniture, that He would visibly dwell in "The Holy Place" and commune with the High Priest as the representative of the Israelites when he entered with blood once a year. The Tabernacle, its furniture, sacrifices, and offerings, was, therefore, the appointed meeting-place of God and sinners. It was only, however, in the Holy Place and through blood that this could be done. In all this the tabernacle was typical of Christ.

God dwells with men in Christ, the meeting place of His appointment. Christ tabernacled in human flesh and was the revelation of God to men, by His pure and holy nature, His perfect and stainless life, His teaching and miracles, His death and resurrection. He was the appointed meeting-place, or reconciliation, because by His life He presented to God that purity of life, thought and action without which God can never dwell with man, and by His death He made an end of sin, and removed the cause and only cause of separation.

In this Tabernacle God dwells with men.

The "Tabernacle of God", "Christ", dwells in the hearts of His people by faith.

The Lord's people regenerated by the Holy Spirit and brought unto union with the divine nature, are the habitation of God through the Spirit. The nature of God, immortality, purity, holiness, love, etc. — becomes their nature and the end towards which their desires and aspirations and prayers tend, though they still possess an old nature of depravity and sin, which in itself separates them from God. The old nature, the flesh, warreth against the new nature of God, and there is a conflict between the in-dwelling of Christ and Satan, but since Christ is the stronger "Grace reigns".

The Tabernacle of God is with men, and He will dwell with them. The church of God when raised from the grave, or redeemed from the land of the enemy, will be without sin, and while still retaining their position as God's creatures, will be in a glorious body, incorruptible, sinless and immortal, and as sin has been removed from their bodies and thoughts and actions by death, or by their living change, there will be no separation, or cause for it. The Tabernacle of God, His abiding presence as Father, Creator, Redeemer and Life of the Church, will dwell with them without visible separation. He will be their God and there will be no cause for interruption of that blest communion. From this visible presence, this "Tabernacle of God", they draw their eternal joys and their hearts are eternally filled with praise. And there shall be no more curse: the curse of separation caused by Adam's fall having been abolished. Neither shall there be any more pain for the former things are passed away. The former things! Sin; pain; sorrow; tears; death, being the curse of separation, were borne by Christ, The Tabernacle of God. This Tabernacle of God is with men and in it God shall dwell with them and He shall be their God and they shall be His people.

DEATH AND THE RESURRECTION.

"For if we believe that Jesus died and rose again, even so them also which sleep in Jesus will God bring with him".

I. Thess. 4.14.*

The outward object of Paul in writing to the Thessalonians was to confirm them in the truth, for though they had believed to their salvation, they were in need of instruction in the truths of the Gospel. He not only desired that they should be safe, but that they should be sound also.

One of the most precious truths which he brings forward is that of the safety and blessedness of those that had fallen asleep in Jesus. This doctrine, although it did not affect their salvation, very much affected their comfort, and through lack of a clear apprehension of this, they lost the most sustaining consolation they could have in the loss of loved ones.

Grace does not eradicate natural ties. There is that real sorrow, that loneliness and vacancy, felt by all that lose dear ones. But though all have this to pass through, for death is no respecter of persons, all have not this comfort. But those whose dear ones fall asleep in Jesus must not sorrow as those who have no hope.

Now the apostle not only holds out this consolation, but shows them the foundation on which it rests. For they might have difficulty in laying hold of this hope; it might seem to their grief-stricken hearts a thing impossible that the corrupting bodies of their dead would ever again be animated or that their souls were indeed with their Lord. "Now!" says the apostle, "You believe that Christ died; that He was as really buried as any of His people. You believe that on the third day He burst the bands of death. Well! He did this as the Head of His people. He died for them and rose again for them. There cannot be a living Head and a dead body; a Saviour in heaven and His people lost in hell. And these two things are so joined together that you cannot believe one without the other. For if you believe that Jesus died and rose again, even so them also that sleep in Jesus will God bring with Him".

There is in the text:-
1. The great object of faith - Jesus died and rose again.
2. The consolation that rests upon it - They which sleep in Jesus, He will bring with Him.

1. The great object of faith
Jesus died. How amazing! The great Creator who upholds all things by the word of His power, submits to the suffering of death.

Observe, He died unto sin; under the curse of the law. He was made a curse for us. This was by imputation, for He knew no sin. "Yet it pleased the Lord to bruise him" (Isaiah 53.10). Who can fathom it? The law demands perfect holiness, perfect conformity. He rendered it. But there was more. Justice holding its fiery sword demands satisfaction for past offences. Will the blood of bulls and of goats satisfy? No. Will the blood of man suffice to

*Preached and afterwards written on the occasion of the death of Mr. Littleton for 52 years Pastor at Crowborough. On 2 January 1921, see pages 29 and 30.

still its flaming vengeance? Never. Wherefore Christ bore its awful stroke. How wonderful! The law thundered its terrors into the heart of the God-Man; the sword awoke against the Man that was God's Fellow and the Shepherd was smitten. But see! The flames of the burning mountain of Sinai are for ever quenched in the blood of Calvary, and the Law's mighty thunders are silenced by the dying words of Christ, "It is finished"

Again: Jesus died and overcame him that had the power of death. Death is an enemy and Christ engaged it in mortal conflict. But whence has death its awful power? What makes it so terrible? *Sin.* The sting of death is sin, and the power of death is the devil. How they came in all their terrible power against the Son of God. But when death laid its icy grip on the Sinners' Substitute, it gripped its own destruction. Christ was the Death of Death and swallowed it up in victory. But He overcame death *through* death, not over it, and by enduring its utmost venom, took the sting away.

But why must the Son of God do this? Could no other man die and so remove the sting? No, because he would be sinful. Now, the sting of death is sin; where there is sin in the nature, there will be the sting untaken away to all eternity. Therefore the apostle says, "who knew no sin" (2. Corinthians 5.21). O! how much of salvation depends on the infinite purity of Christ.

Again. He died actually, and absolutely. It was not a lapsing into unconsciousness but a real severing of soul and body, so that the human body was inanimate and would in the ordinary way have become corrupt. His spirit He committed to His Father and His body was buried in the place where there was a garden. How many of His people had been laid in their graves before that, and how many since! But that night the Lord of Glory was as truly buried as any of them

"Where should the dying members rest,
But with their dying Head?"

Watts

It was necessary that the Captain of our salvation should pass through this. Not only to salvation, but that He might be a sympathetic High Priest. He knows what dying pains are, for He cried "unto him that was able to save him from death" (Hebrews 5.7). And now there is no place that believers can come into, where Jesus has not been before, not even the grave itself.

But He rose again. "Jesus died and rose again". He not only went into the grave, but out again, and herein lies the foundation of that great gospel truth "Justification". "and was raised again for our justification" Romans 4.25. Death is the penalty of sin, but when He rose from the dead, there was therefore, no penalty left, nor can there be one stain left on the Church of Christ. He was the first-fruits of them that slept. If the first-fruits rose again, the remainder must follow in their season. And the same power that raised up Christ from the dead, shall quicken their mortal bodies also, in His heavenly image. And He ascended on high. Not as He was before all creation, ever with the Father, but in that human body wherein He was one with His people, not only in covenant relationship, but in a participation of nature. For though the Son of God had ever been in the realms of Glory, the Son of Man had not, until the cloud received Him and He ascended a Victor.

147

It was His right that Heaven should open to Him. So the 24th Psalm — "Open ye the gates". But to whom shall these golden gates be opened? Sin had closed them; the justice of God had barred them; His holiness had bolted them. "Who is this King of Glory? The Lord mighty in battle". And before Him, bearing in His body the marks of that awful conflict, and clothed in a vesture dipped in blood, the gates open. There is no sin left to close them. Justice draws back the bolts and Holiness the bars. The King of Glory enters amidst the praises of Heaven. And did they close again? Never! They are open still and the ransomed souls of His people enter therein when death effects the separation. Stephen in his dying moments saw this and committed his spirit into the Saviour's keeping. But the great question is:- Have we any interest in this? Are our sins put away by this sacrifice? Are the heavens open to us? Shall we enter those glorious portals? Where is the evidence to be found? In our own hearts. We must turn our eyes inward. But what is the evidence? *FAITH. Faith. If we believe*. But what faith is this? Is it a natural assent? Is it of an historical kind? No. No. It must be living, acting, moving. But how does it act and where does it move? To the cross of Christ. It derives its life from Christ's death. It acts on that; pleads it before God; clings to it as a drowning man to a lifebelt. It moves to it and the believer (for he is a believer) is favoured sometimes with precious nearness to it and can say,

> "Here it is I find my heaven,
> While upon the Lamb I gaze"   *Allen & Batty*

Everyone that has been redeemed by blood, comes to the blood. O! what a procession of guilty, burdened and sin-sick sinners there has been to that place called Golgotha! And none ever went from there to Hell. Jesus Christ went from the Cross to the Crown, and all His people have gone the same way.

2. The consolation "So them also that sleep in Jesus will God bring with him".

Death, though vanquished and overcome by Christ and for all who are in Christ, is nevertheless, at times, very terrible and fills the soul with very gloomy forebodings. Even Paul himself did not wish to be unclothed, but clothed upon. Nor is there anything sinful in this. But the Apostle shows that death to a believer is only a sleep. In Revelation 14.13: "Blessed are the dead which die in the Lord". Now, to die in the Lord is to sleep in Jesus and we can see why it is compared to sleep when we consider that:-

a. *There is no wrath, curse or sting in it.*
He is not cut off by God's wrath, but taken home. It is not the justice of God taking vengeance on him but "My Beloved is gone down into his garden .... to gather lilies" (Song of Sol. 6.2). Not hurled into the eternal abode of misery, but brought into the haven of his soul's desire. And there is no sting, for his sins are forgiven and

> "If sin be pardoned, I'm secure;
> Death has no sting beside;"   *Watts.*

O! what an awful thing to enter that changeless eternity loaded with unforgiven sin. That is the worm that dieth not, and the fire that is not quenched is God's anger against it. But there is nothing of this in the death of a believer. How blessed, to meet that God, whose love and mercy we have felt here below. This surely must be to sleep in Jesus. We do not dread our sleep, it is necessary to us. So this is necessary before we can see His face in righteousness.

b. *Also it is a sleep because it is rest.* "That they may rest from their labours" (Rev. 14.13). Jesus said of Lazarus that he "sleepeth" (John 11.11). They rest from that inward conflict between the flesh and the spirit; from the pains and weakness of a poor suffering body. We all know what suffering days and sleepless nights are, in our measure. And how sweet and relieving rest is afterwards. How much of this often accompanies the taking down of this tabernacle. But these are a believer's last pains. They all end when his breath leaves his body. "For so he giveth his beloved sleep" (Psalm 127.2). Besides they are not alone when they enter the valley of death, for Christ never leaves His people to finish off alone. The arms of everlasting love are never more beneath them than when they commit their souls into His keeping. If the sustaining arms of dear ones are so comforting to our bodies, what must the arms of Christ be to our souls? And must it not be rest to die in this way? O! to feel Christ beneath when we sink down into death! We shall find it to be rest indeed.

c. *It is a sleep because there is no end of existence in it.* We do not cease to live naturally when we sleep. Therefore the Apostle says "Absent from the body, and to be present with the Lord" (2. Cor. 5.8). There is no end of existence in it. The scriptures show no intermediate state between the absence of the body and the presence with the Lord. Christ said to the dying thief, "To-day", (this very day that thou art hanging on the cross) "shalt thou be with me in paradise" (Luke 23.43). We all know the mournful preparations that follow; the sorrowful days, but the departed ones know nothing of that. No sooner do their eyes become dim and clouded and darkened, than the glorious vision of Him whom "having not seen" (1. Pet. 1.8) we love, unfolds to view. And as earth recedes, so Heaven, that glorious Heaven, draws near, and it is all over. He is "With Christ".

d. *It is a sleep because there will be an awakening.* "For the Lord himself shall descend from heaven with a shout, with the voice of the archangel, and with the trump of God: and the dead in Christ shall rise first". (1. Thess. 4.16). Their graves will open. They have been there long, but the great trumpet will reach them. Death cannot hold them any longer, and they will come forth. Not as they were laid there, poor corrupting bodies, sown in corruption, but in the image of Christ. "For this corruptible must put on incorruption" (1. Cor. 15.53) and "Who shall change our vile body, that it may be fashioned like unto his glorious body" (Philippians 3.21). But it will not be an awakening to those things from which they rested. That is all gone "for the former things are passed away" (Rev. 21.4). "Well", says the Apostle, "they that sleep in Jesus" — this is to be well laid in the grave.

It remains only to make some application of these thoughts to the departure of Mr. Littleton. We may be assured that these things are blessedly true of him. There was no sting in his death. It was a real entering into rest. Almost, if not quite the last time he was in the Chapel, he said to

149

me and some more friends at the Chapel door, "I want rest". He is with Christ. Long he served Him. Now he has received his reward. The journey is ended and the conflict won. He has laid down the sword and wears the crown. And that body that was buried will rise again, according to this word. He has rested from his labours. You know how faithfully he preached. How he watched for your souls as one that must give an account. Now that is all over.

To those that have lost him as a relative, here lies the consolation: "Ye sorrow not, even as others which have no hope" (I. Thess. 4.13.). To those who have lost him as a pastor, remember how he sought your spiritual welfare and endeavoured to keep you in union. Seek, as you are able, to follow on. He would say "Amen" to this were he here. Remember his words when he was with you. He has gone, but the precious truths he maintained are still the same. And when we come to our appointed end, may our end be like his.

THE PREACHING OF THE CROSS

"For the preaching of the cross is to them that perish foolishness; but unto us which are saved it is the power of God".

1 Corinthians 1.18.*

.......Human reason stumbles at this, and is offended. But living faith sees the glory of God, the wisdom of God, the power of God and the love of God. This wisdom "none of the princes of this world knew: for had they known it, they would not have *crucified the Lord of glory*" (I. Cor 2.8).

The second thing that brings out the contrasting of God's wisdom and human reason is, 'The preaching of The Gospel'.

Here again, man would fit men to preach with high education, select men with great gifts and endeavour to make the preaching of the Gospel successful through the aid of men's ability. They conceive the idea that the gospel of God's grace can be made more attractive if set off with natural polish, so that to-day the churches are filled with men who have nothing more than human wisdom to go with; nothing more than human wisdom to preach; so that the Cross is made of none effect through their tradition. Such preaching gives no offence, but on the contrary, God works so opposite to men that He "chooses the weak things of the world to confound the things which are mighty" (I. Cor. 1.27) and the great end of God, both in the salvation of men and the preaching of the gospel is to bring glory to His name. And the great reason why such worldly-foolish means are used is "that no flesh should glory in His presence" (I Cor. 1.29). In the text there is

1. *What is, and what is not, meant by the Cross*
2. *What the Preaching of the Cross is*

*The first page (or pages) of these handwritten sermon notes is missing but the content of the remainder so clearly expresses the constant emphasis of his ministry that it has to be included.

3. *Why it is foolishness to them that perish*
4. *Why it is the power of God to them that are saved.*

1. By "the Cross" is *not* meant any reference to the material wood on which the sinless body of Christ was crucified since that could effect nothing. If that were actually in existence, it would not bring peace or pardon or life or eternal salvation, which are the principal fruits of the cross of Christ. How fruitless then, must be any worship or religion that consists in adoration of a material image of the Cross.

By "the Cross" is *not* meant that which follows the outward profession of the name of Christ. Of which the Lord said "Let him take up his cross and follow Me". Herein believers in some measure enter into the fellowship of Christ's sufferings, but this fellowship is a fruit of the cross of Christ.

By "the Cross" *is* meant the sufferings and death of the Son of God in human nature, together with the doctrines that emanate therefrom which are called the doctrines of the cross.

The cross of Christ was divinely appointed by the eternal purpose of God, divinely agreed by the Son of God in the Covenant of Grace. Wherefore He is said to be "the Lamb slain from the foundation of the world" (Rev. 13.8). The cross of Christ was willingly submitted to: "Lo, I come.....to do thy will, O God" (Hebrews 10.7). He was straitened till it was accomplished. His enemies were not more willing to put Him to death than He was to undergo it. The ardent prayer of Christ in Gethsemane does not show any unwillingness to drink the cup of suffering but only the reality of His human nature and the greatness of that suffering.

The justice of God is clearly displayed in the Cross of Christ. *How great* since it required such an appeasing as this. *How infinite* since it required an infinite sacrifice. *How holy* since nothing could satisfy it except one so holy as the Son of God.

The cross of Christ means the shame and ignominy with which it was endured. It was a death for malefactors. Therefore He despised the shame for the joy that was set before Him. The salvation of the Church was of so great a joy to Christ that He endured the shame of the Cross.

The high priest, the Jews, the Roman soldiers united against Him, "Many bulls have compassed me: strong bulls of Bashan have beset me round" (Psalm 22.12): "they pierced my hands and my feet" (Ps. 22.16). And in this He was supported by the Holy Spirit; therefore it is said that He "through the eternal Spirit offered himself without spot to God" (Hebrews 9.14).

The Cross, as intended in the text, means, therefore, the bodily and spiritual sufferings which Christ endured. The more we are led into this mystery, and are enabled by faith to perceive herein the purpose of God in the salvation of the Church, so we shall enter into the Apostle's words "God forbid that I should glory save in the cross of our Lord Jesus Christ".

2. Notice in the next point: What the preaching of the Cross is. It was the will of God that the doctrines of the Cross should be preached to all the world. Nor did He lack ministers, for He called a Peter from his nets, Paul from his persecuting career and others from their callings, and divinely fitted them, and spiritually qualified them for this work.
Notice how Paul preached the Cross:

Preaching Peace

a. That He who suffered thereon was the Son of God (Acts 9.20). This they did not believe: "If thou be the Son of God etc.". Herein lays a foundation truth of the Gospel. If He that was crucified be the Son of God there is divine virtue, divine efficacy, infinite comprehensiveness in it. Herein it is that the death of One atones for so many; herein is such a firm and solid foundation of the Church's hope and glory.

b. He preached the Cross in this, that there is forgiveness of sins thereby. "Through this man is preached unto you the forgiveness of sins:" (Acts 13.38). There is nothing so necessary to enter Heaven as this. Sin forms an insuperable barrier between a sinner and God; brings him under eternal wrath and condemnation; and this felt in the experience, brings fear of death, judgment and eternal misery. The preaching of the Cross and forgiveness thereby is "the trumpet". "And it shall come to pass in that day, that the great trumpet shall be blown, and they shall come which were ready to perish..." (Isaiah 27.13)

c. As the foundation of a believer's hope, confidence, peace and future glory. This theme should be the very essence of a gospel ministry. This will be profitable and bring liberty; besides, nothing else will stand for preacher or hearer in the day of judgment.

3. In the third place this preaching is to some foolishness.

Since men are sunk in ruin, why do they not at once grasp at this, the only way of salvation?. Because:-

a. *They do not know that they are lost,* nor see nor feel their need of salvation. Therefore the preaching of the Cross appears useless. They do not see why the apostle should undergo so many privations for what seems nothing more than to publish an opinion.

b. *They have no faith.* "the word preached did not profit them, not being mixed with faith in them that heard it" (Heb. 4.2). Faith operates in the heart and co-operates with the preaching of the Cross. Otherwise, as in this case, it is all external. Observe, there must be something more than mere hearing or the most faithful sermon will be in itself ineffective.

c. It leaves no room for human wisdom, power or strength; lays the knife at the root of all human attainments. Man's pride is in his wisdom. This preaching makes the wisdom of this world, foolishness. They glory in their strength; this makes it utter weakness.

d. It is foolishness because it insists on separation from the things of this world. They who glory in the Cross are crucified to this world and this world to them. They who would carry this world to the verge of heaven and then effect an exchange will see nothing but foolishness in this preaching.

Notice the stamp upon all to whom this preaching is foolishness "them that are lost". Fatal mark, the very stamp of condemnation if we see no glory, no wisdom, no preciousness in the preaching of the Cross. God Himself stamps upon us this condemnation.

4. Notice in the fourth and last point, why the preaching of the Cross is to them that are saved "the power of God".

Herein lays a real evidence of our salvation if we can say that it has been powerful to us.

a. It is one of the chief means used by God to convey into the hearts of

152

sinners, the powerful effects of the Cross. The Cross of Christ is very powerful in itself. There was the great battle between the powers of Heaven and of Hell; there the Captain of our Salvation engaged the enemies of the Church. How they assaulted the Son of God; how they wounded Him. He looked for some to help and there was none.

> "Many hands were raised to wound him;
> None would interpose to save".

How powerfully they assaulted Him. If He be overcome the Church is for ever lost; hell swallows the whole human race; but He overcame. He conquered though He fell and in that dreadful night did all the powers of hell destroy. Therefore the 24th Psalm "Lift up your heads, O ye gates .... Who is this King of glory? The Lord strong and mighty, the Lord mighty in battle .... He is the King of glory". Also in the Revelation "On his head were many crowns" (Rev. 19.12).

Now the same foes that were defeated by the Lord Jesus, hold the souls of His people under their sway. They are held captive at the Devil's will, so that they need to be overcome again. But the first victory ensures the second.

b. Because it is accompanied by the Spirit of power. How useless is preaching without this. How we may speak strongly and encouragingly and truthfully, and we may think powerfully, and yet there are no results; sinners are not converted nor the Lord's people strengthened. In fact, the ministry is only like a cloud without water, under which souls may get as dry and hard as the cracking earth in summer. But when the Spirit of power attends it, how the word, and the Cross of Christ, as held forth to sin-burdened sinners, how powerfully it works. How it turns a heart as hard as a millstone into a melting spring of love to Jesus Christ, and raises up hope in the mind of one who feels ready to sink into eternal despair. It is the trumpet that shall sound when they that were ready to perish shall come. It shall turn their hell into heaven. To this precious experience I set my own seal.

d. It is powerful because it works powerful results. We, who have heard this preaching, should ask ourselves what effects it has had on us. The Apostle said, "To the one we are the savour of death unto death; and to the other the savour of life unto life" (2 Corinthians 2.16). Observe, every gospel sermon will be either life or death to us. Christ said, "The words that I speak unto you, they are spirit, and they are life" (John 6.63) and "the word that I have spoken, the same shall judge him in the last day" (John 12.48).

But what does it so powerfully work?

It *works life*. Nothing else does. The Law thunders curse and death. Our own righteousness works death eternal for it can never stand in the judgment; our own wisdom will never atone for our own sin. What then can work life? Why! the Cross of Christ.

> "Death's within thee, all about thee,
> But the remedy's without thee;
> See it in thy Saviour's blood".

It was when Moses lifted up the brazen serpent, that they who were bitten could look and live. Well, the ministry should be like the pole, which is only useful as far as it holds forth Jesus Christ, the Sin-healer in the form of the sinner. But that must be powerful which can work life in the hearts of sinners so very much dead.

Again it *maintains life*. The life of grace gets down to a spark. Deadness of spirit; carnality of mind; pride, that greatest of all enemies; love of the world, are like so much water on the fire of grace, and so effectually does it damp, that our efforts to stand against these things are powerless. Who does not sometimes fear that eternal life will go out? But what can stand against these just opponents and maintain life in the soul in spite of all? I answer from my own experience — the power of the Cross; whether it be in preaching or hearing, and in this way the preaching of the Cross is the power of God.

Again, it works *felt reconciliation*. Not real reconciliation for that was effected once and for all in the death of God's Son. But we can only safely know if we were reconciled then, by the realisation of it now. What a great thing! Heaven is opened to receive me to eternal mansions if I am reconciled to God. What a precious experience; how deep; how real; how abiding; how solid! Herein lies an evidence if a man is sent to preach — does his ministry work these solid things in the hearers, or does it merely set off his natural abilities? Herein, also, is a real test for hearers — do they merely like *the man*? Are they interested; do they say "He is a promising young man"? Or do they enter into this, and can they set their seal to these God-given evidences?

Observe again, it works *peace in the conscience and comfort in the heart*. But it does this in a discriminating way. It does not cry, "Peace," where there is no peace. It does not give comfort in the face of eternal misery. It points to the foundation of peace and to the source of comfort, "The Cross of Christ". It shows to whom this peace and comfort belongs.

Suppose there is a man who is a believer and who is in much darkness of mind and enduring temptation, joined perhaps with outward trials. And then within there is an accusing conscience, raking up past sins, seeming like a great white throne in his own heart or as Bunyan says "Mr. Recorder". He feels that his religion is all pretence, that all he may have said will rise up in judgment against him. Comfort he has none. He can take none in himself or in reading even God's Word. Where can he find such peace as shall quiet his conscience? what shall speak peace to the restless sea that he feels within, or where is such comfort as that he can look on all his outward troubles with contentment? Well! Suppose he hears the preaching of the Cross, and the merit of Christ's atonement, the cleansing power of His precious blood, the gracious invitations of the Gospel reach his outward ear, and then enter into his soul, with such sweetness and power, as side by side with his own sin, he sees the blood of Christ and the one so much abounds over the other. And as conscience speaks loud and condemning, the blood of Christ speaks better things than that of Abel. As he feels that sin abounds, he begins to see how grace abounds over it, and divine love begins to operate in his heart, and love within begins to be attracted back again to Christ and the fear of death is so far removed as that he would depart and be with Christ which is far better. This is powerful working.

Again, it works *holy confidence*. "We are always confident," fears are gone while the power of the Gospel is felt. Confident of our acceptance with God; confident that that which He has begun, He will perfect at last

"Thou, Lord, wilt carry on,
And perfectly perform,
The work Thou hast begun
In me, a sinful worm".

Lastly, see the stamp the Holy Spirit puts on this kind of hearing. To them that are saved it is the power of God. Saved, eternally saved. The preaching of the Cross never works these powerful things in the hearts of lost sinners. "Lost" is the fatal mark on the one; "Saved" is the blessed mark on the other. Saved from sin; from the sulphurous flames of endless misery; from the abode of devils and lost spirits. Saved to the realms of endless glory, endless happiness, endless holiness. O! may the power of the Cross be the power of my heart's experience!

PUBLISH THE NAME OF THE LORD.

The last Sermon preached by Mr. S. Delves.
Forest Fold Baptist Chapel.*

"Because I will publish the name of the LORD; ascribe ye greatness unto our God. He is the Rock, his work is perfect; for all his ways are judgment; a God of truth and without iniquity, just and right is he."

Deut. 32. 3-4.

It has occurred to me, in pondering over this subject and its context in this chapter, that the chapter itself may hardly seem to bear out the expectations that such a sublime commencement would suggest to the mind. In fact the chapter is mostly devoted to a prophetical foreknowledge of the perverse ways of Israel, and how provoking those ways were in the sight of God, and what solemn judgments such provocation would bring upon them. Now it might be thought, "Where in all this is the doctrine that drops as the rain with such a refreshing? And where is the speech so sweet and so sacred as to distil as the dew, in all these solemn denunciations?". But then we must remember, as I said when I commenced the whole subject, that Moses in this chapter is speaking prophetically, and prophetically of the gospel, and particularly of the gospel as it would be proclaimed by the lips of the Lord Jesus Christ Himself, and subsequently from the lips of all Spirit-anointed preachers of the same truth. But this anticipates at the same time that that gospel would be in general rejected by the nation of Israel. What, for instance, could be more expressive of that than the sixth verse? "Do ye thus requite the LORD, O foolish people and unwise? is not he thy Father that hath brought thee? hath he not made thee, and established thee?" Now what a base requital it was of the goodness of God in sending the promised Messiah, His only-begotten Son, to that nation, that He should be despised and rejected by those very people! So that it all fits together, really. The commencement is a beautiful and sublime anticipation of the gospel and the

*This sermon was preached 22 January 1978, evidently in great weakness only six weeks before he died.

preaching of it, followed by the sad rejection of the gospel by that nation of the Jews.

Now there can be no mistake in my giving you this interpretation of this chapter, because in the chapter in Romans that was read to us just now, in which the rejection of this gospel is expressly set forth, it is written, "First Moses saith, I will provoke you to jealousy by them that are no people"(Romans 10.19). Well, where did Moses say that? In this very chapter. So there can be no mistake with the interpretation I am giving of this prophetical Scripture.

But the Lord has always had a people to whom the gospel has been made life and power, even in the darkest days. And although Israel as a nation rejected the gospel, yet there was a remnant, as the apostle says, that did not reject the gospel, but on whose hearts it had exactly the same effect the first verse describes. And why was there a remnant? Why were there any at all that received, in faith and love, the blessed gospel of Jesus Christ? Let men say what they will, the plain answer is this: it was a "remnant according to the election of grace." (Romans 11.5). And if there had been no election of grace, there would have been no remnant.

Well, I must not take time this morning upon this matter, but I felt that I must just point it out to you, because you might think if you read down the chapter that it hardly bears out the sublime and beautiful commencement of it.

Let us now, then, turn to the text. "Because I will publish the name of the Lord; ascribe ye greatness unto our God." Now it was because of this publishing of the name of the Lord that the doctrine and the speech had this gracious effect. For whatever is published, other than the name of the Lord and all that that most blessed name implies, contains, and conveys; any other doctrine but the doctrine of the gospel of Jesus Christ, will never have any gracious effect upon the hearts of men.

But it comes in my way this morning in speaking upon this word, to offer you a few considerations with regard to the publishing of the name of the Lord — in other words, to set before you what *the preaching of the gospel* really is; because there is a great deal of misunderstanding about this very matter. Preaching is the main appointment of the gospel dispensation. That is very evident by the emphasis that is laid upon it in the New Testament; there is very little said there about the other ordinances except enough to establish them as being divinely-appointed ones, but there is no salvation in those ordinances. But the preaching of the gospel is the means, under the blessing of God, of salvation. Now there are three words which express the true nature of preaching the Word and the first is in our text, *publishing* it: "Because I will publish the name of the Lord." Another equally expressive word is, to *proclaim* it: that is, to set forth boldly and unrepentantly the truth of the gospel. The other word, of course, is to *preach*. Now to publish, to proclaim and to preach are three words that express the true nature of preaching the gospel.

Now I do not want to introduce into the sermon this morning anything of a controversial nature, but sometimes just a word or two dropped by the way may be acceptable - at least you will know where I stand in this matter. Now there has been for many years, and is still, a good deal said about the 'gospel offer' - in other words, offering the gospel to all men indiscriminately. Now with some, this gospel offer is almost an integral part of their ministry. But I never feel that I can agree with it, because for one thing you never find such a word used in the Scripture with regard to the preaching of the Word. You take a Cruden's Concordance and look down to see how often the word 'offer' appears in the New Testament. You will find it appears a great number of times but never once in connection with the preaching of the gospel. So that I do not feel myself that the term 'gospel offer' is Scriptural, and what is more, I think it may be very misleading. I do not come before you this morning to offer Jesus Christ to you, but, as the Lord may help me, plainly to proclaim His name in the richness, fulness, blessedness and freeness of it; and that there is salvation in His name to every one that believeth, whosoever he may be. It is said sometimes that if we do not stand for the 'gospel offer' we limit the freeness and extent of the gospel. Now with that I do not agree for one moment. The fulness and extent of the gospel is expressed in words like these: "For God so loved the world, that He gave His only begotten Son, that *whosoever* believeth in Him should not perish, but have everlasting life." (John 3.16). Now what could make the gospel more free to all, with ears to hear it and hearts to respond to it, than a word like that? And again it is said, "Whosoever believeth in Him shall receive the remission of sins." (Acts 10.43). Whosoever, whosoever! Let no one say, "There is no hope for me in a word like that", because there is, if any have hearts to respond to it. And remember that Jesus said, "Him that cometh to me I will in no wise cast out;" and that means, as John Bunyan says somewhere, any 'him' that comes, any 'him' that comes (John 6.37). Now I would ask any fair-minded hearer, "If we set these things forward in their Scriptural connection, in whatever way do we limit the freeness of the gospel?" (But now that is enough about that).

What was more upon my mind to mention this morning before I attempt to get a little deeper into the substance of the text is this: there is something special about the preaching of the gospel that does not apply to anything else. And that is this: the preaching of the gospel is directed to the *heart*. The ultimate objective of the gospel, and the preaching of it, is the hearts of men. Now if the word of the gospel does not reach their hearts, then it has failed to convey any real spiritual good to their souls. For it is "with the heart man believeth unto righteousness" (Romans 10.10); therefore the Word must reach his heart.

Now when I say this, I am not by-passing the necessity of the understanding being enlightened with regard to the truth and teaching of the Word. You know I have said to you sometimes before, that the understanding to the heart is like the porch to the house. There is no entrance into the house except through the porch; so there is no entrance of the Word into the heart if the understanding remains blinded and unseeing, as it is written, "having the understanding darkened...... through the ignorance that is in them" (Eph. 4.18). Now the natural understanding of men, by various causes, is very dark with regard to a spiritual discernment of the holy nature of the truths of the gospel. But there is such a thing as having the understanding enlightened, and the Word getting no farther than that: in other words, the Word entering into the porch but not entering into the house. That may well be. But still, instructing the understanding, though it is a most important part of publishing or proclaiming the gospel, is not its ultimate end, which is to reach the heart. And so you will remember that when the Lord drew near to the disciples on that journey to Emmaus, He opened the Scriptures to their understanding and later opened their understanding that they might understand the Scriptures (Luke 24: 32,45). Very good. But the word went deeper than that. So that afterwards they did not say, "How wonderfully we understood those Scriptures!" Nay, brethren. "Did not our heart burn within us?" "Did not our heart burn within us?" - the holy fire of the Word reached through the understanding into their hearts.

Now, my friends, it is with your hearts I have to deal as a minister. But there is a great difficulty. When the Word enters the heart, it meets with a strong barrier. It is easier for the Word to enter the understanding and instruct it, than to enter into the heart and awaken it with conviction, and bring forth faith to believe it. For the barrier in the natural hearts of men against the word of the gospel is *exceedingly* strong. It is Satan's great bulwark of hardness of heart so that the Word of God never penetrates through that barrier into the heart. Sometimes this barrier in the heart is more or less latent; it is just an unconcern; and no words can get through it. Sometimes it is an opposition; the Word stirs up enmity, and no power that is in any minister or any man can overcome that barrier. What then? Now here comes in the Holy Ghost, brethren; here comes in the Holy Ghost. It is the Holy Spirit's work to make the Word so effectual that notwithstanding the barrier against it in the human heart through unbelief or the love of sin or what not, the Word penetrates through the barrier. Now when the Holy Spirit makes the Word penetrate through the barrier, then it reaches the heart, its true objective. O it is useless to preach the gospel without the Holy Spirit! It really is. For no wit nor wisdom nor might, no way of persuasion however pathetic, no warning however solemn, no instruction however true in itself, will get through that barrier.

Permit me to say this: blessed be God for everyone here in whose heart that barrier has been broken down, and the Word of God has had its entrance! Because where the Word of God has its entrance, it invariably brings salvation with it. And so runs that beautiful word that was read this morning: "How beautiful upon the mountains are the feet of him that bringeth good tidings, that publisheth peace; that bringeth good tidings of good, that publisheth salvation" (Isa. 52.7; Rom. 10.15). And very often one of the very first effects of the breaking down of the barrier of the heart by the Holy Spirit, is that the heart becomes convinced of the sinfulness of that barrier itself - of its unconcern, its unbelief, its disdain, and perhaps its scorn for the gospel. Often one of the first effects is conviction of the sinfulness of that condition which was a barrier against the Word of truth. So I say again, Blessed be God if that barrier has been broken down in our hearts! For nothing but His grace – His sovereign, powerful, effectual grace — could ever have done it. Nothing could ever have done it but the power of the grace of God operated by the Holy Spirit. Well now, I felt I wanted to say that about preaching this morning, because of course it comes within the scope of my text: "Because I will publish" — preach, proclaim, declare, set forth — "the name of the Lord."

Now we may well meditate for a few moments upon the significance of this expression: "*the name of the Lord.*" Now by the name of the Lord we must understand two things, or rather two features of the same blessed thing. And first of all, by the name of the Lord we must understand the holy, majestic and blessed *perfections of the divine nature itself.* The name of the Lord contains the expression of all that God Himself is. Now Moses was in a special position to be able to proclaim the name of the Lord because the Lord had proclaimed His name to Moses. As you read towards the end of the book of Exodus, Moses entreated of the Lord to show him His glory. That was a prayer impossible to answer at that time but the Lord passed by, we read, and proclaimed His name. And what was His name? "The Lord... merciful and gracious, longsuffering, and abundant in goodness and truth" (Ex. 34.6).

Now every divine perfection is in the name of the Lord. Where you read in the Old Testament, or perhaps in the New, the sacred name of God, it means the divine Nature itself; the divine Nature is God; God is the divine Nature. The divine Nature is a Nature of infinite purity, holiness, majesty, wisdom, power, goodness, love and justice — we must not exclude that. But the divine Nature dwells in three divine Persons — the Father, the Son, and the Holy Spirit. Now these three divine Persons are one divine Nature, one God. But the divine Nature dwells in three divine Persons; of these divine Persons, One became Man, and was born into this world of ours; and there was given to Him the name that will always be very precious, *the name of Jesus.* Now all that God is, Jesus is; all that Jesus is in the divine Nature, God is. So to publish the name of the Lord is to publish the name of the Lord Jesus Christ, because it was expressly said of God concerning Jesus Christ, "My name is in him" (Ex. 23.21). Now here is something, had we but spiritual discernment of it, and did we but feel the holy and solemn nature of it, which would fill us with wonder and worship; that is, that the Lord Jesus Christ, in our very nature, is all that God is, in the divine Nature.

So first then, to publish the name of the Lord is to publish it as it is in the Person of Jesus Christ. Of course, Moses would not have seen it in quite that clear light; but now in the clear light of the gospel it seems plain enough. To publish the name of the Lord is to publish His name in the very Person of the Lord Jesus Christ. And He is very near to us, near to us in our nature. In Jesus Christ every divine perfection is near to us, in the gospel. The divine perfections considered in themselves are awesome, sublime. They seem O so far, far beyond us, too holy for us to comprehend, too majestic for us to realise! O so far above us in our limited human capacity! But now in Jesus Christ they are revealed to us in such a way that we can publish His name believingly and thankfully and say, "Yes, this wonderful God is my Saviour in Jesus." He it was, in the Person of His dear Son, who shed His precious blood to atone for sinners. He it was who wrought out a righteousness so perfect and so complete, which is imputed unto all that believe. O brethren, it is impossible to express what the name of the Lord really is! For sweetness, for richness, for fulness, for tenderness, for nearness — O brethren, it warms my very heart to proclaim His name this morning!

"Because I will publish the name of the Lord". And why publish the name of the Lord but that your hearts should be drawn out to Him? That the Word should so reach your hearts, the barrier of which I have spoken having been broken down, that now you can say, "Yes, I can see it, and not only see it in my understanding but I can feel it in my heart. Jesus Christ is just that Person I want, just the Saviour, just the Redeemer. He is so mighty to save, so compassionate to sinners, so receptive of all that come to Him. His heart is so large it will embrace all who penitently cast themselves upon His arms. He will receive all; His heart is great enough for that." That is why we publish the name of the Lord, that the sweet savour of His name should be shed abroad in our midst and in our hearts by the Holy Spirit. So you read in one of the epistles, that the savour of the knowledge of the Lord Jesus Christ is shed abroad by us in every place. (2 Cor. 2.14)

Now of course my ministry must be drawing to its end, and I do feel that the best and most satisfying thing to me of all that could be said of my preaching is that there has been a savour of the knowledge of the Lord Jesus Christ in it, and that it has been shed abroad in your hearts in this place. O what can I say to win your hearts for Jesus Christ this morning? O Holy Spirit, do Thou do it!

"Because I will publish the name of the Lord." As I say, publish anything else, and there is nothing for poor, seeking, needy sinners, for hungry hearts, for helpless people. Publish anything but the name of the Lord and it will leave them high and dry. They will say, "Oh, it was a beautiful sermon, but there was nothing in it for me. It never met my case."

"Ascribe ye *greatness* unto our God." Now there is a beautiful combination in these matters between a sweet and gracious freedom with regard to Jesus Christ, and a reverential awe at the greatness of His nature. So that while we publish the name of the Lord in all its freeness and suitability and richness, we still ascribe greatness to our God. O, He is a great God! Who is a God like unto our God? Who amongst the sons of the mighty can be compared unto Him? (Ps. 89.6). What a comparison the psalmist makes in one of the psalms (Ps. 115) between the gods of the heathen and the true God! Consider the gods of the heathen; they are weak, helpless gods. They have eyes, but they cannot see their worshippers; they have ears but they cannot hear. No, not even the priests of Baal, who cried out from morning till evening, "O Baal, hear us!" But there was none that answered, because Baal had got ears that could not hear. O, our God is not like that! O what ears He has to hear our poor cries! What power He has to appear for us and help us! What eyes He has to discern our needy condition and relieve us! O there is no god like to our God! And our God is in Jesus Christ. You know we read, "there are gods many, and lords many" (I Cor. 8.5). And so I feel with regard to the coming into our country of what is commonly called a multi-racial society. Now these represent different religions, and different religions have different gods. But there is no god like our God, the God of our Lord Jesus Christ, the Christian's God. Oh, there is no god like that God! "Ascribe ye greatness unto our God." Do it, brethren from your hearts.

For one thing, we ascribed great *wisdom* to our God. "There is no searching of His understanding" (Isa. 40.28). "His ways are past finding out" (Rom. 11.33). We ascribe great *power* to our God, both in creation and in grace. He has power to create worlds, and He has power to save sinful individual souls. We ascribe greatness of power to our God. And, lastly, we ascribe great *love* to our God. "For his great love, wherewith he loved us, even when we were dead in sins". (Eph. 2.4-5). O the greatness of that love! Its height — no one can ascend to the height of it; its depth – no one can fathom its depth; its length — no one can measure its infinite degree; its breadth – no one can say to what distance it embraces.

Pardon me, my friends, my strength has gone.

"Because I will publish the name of the Lord: ascribe ye greatness unto our God."